Meditations on God and Children

John C. Orndorff

Meditations on God and Children

John C. Orndorff

Published by:

pensive books
springfield, tn

ISBN: 978-1-893213-15-9

All photographs by John C. Orndorff, Debora M. Orndorff and Mary Allen

To our grandchildren

Tristan, Brandon, Kensly, JJ, Ella, Blakely, Boden, Ila Ruth, and Bristol

The richness of your life will be measured according to the depth of your relationship with God.

And

To my Mom, Ruth Orndorff

And

In memory of my Dad, William I. "Bill" Orndorff

Table of Contents

Read This First!

Debi, my wife, told me several years ago that she did not read the introduction to books. This comment troubled me as I use the introductions in my writing to, well, introduce my subject and explain a few things. The introduction is where I open my soul to the world. Starters of this nature are meant to enhance the reader's understanding of why writers take the time to write and provide an idea of what the reader can hope to gain from reading it. However, I do understand those who wish to get to the meat of the subject, and I grudgingly accept that. Therefore, this is not an introduction; I just want you to read it first.

This is an expanded version of *From the Mouths of Babes: Growing Closer to God through Children*, which was published in 2017. I have added eight chapters: Why Children?, Watching Father God Work, Nimrod the Mighty Hunter, When Life Gets Out of Control, Written For Us, Not Now, The Small Things, and When There Is No One at the Door. I need to get one thing straight here, and that has to do with the inspiration for this book. This is the work of the Holy Spirit teaching and guiding me. I wanted to write a book on spiritual warfare, but the Lord would not allow me to write it. The result is that for me, when I go back and read these pages, it is like I never wrote them.

Debi and I have been blessed with three wonderful and talented children, John (CJ), Michael and Mary. As other parents will agree, most of the time they bring us much joy in many ways. We also have nine really neat grandchildren: Tristan, Brandon, Kensly, JJ, Ella, Blakely, Boden, Ila Ruth, and Bristol. From the beginning of child rearing, I've been learning through my children. I just haven't taken the time to write about what I was learning. Now, in obedience to God's direction (I really do believe my Heavenly Father wanted me to write this), I'm taking that time. As I have worked on this short book, originally entitled Lessons Through JJ and Ella, it has become an opportunity to learn even more than during the actual experiences with JJ and Ella.

As I began preparing these thoughts, I did so based on Matthew 7:9-11, "What sort of parent would give his or her child a stone rather than bread or hand him or her a serpent rather than a fish? If you, corrupt as you are, know to provide good things to your children, then don't you think your Heavenly Father will provide good things to those who ask?" My impression is that our Heavenly Father has the same parental feelings for us as we have for our children, just multiplied many times higher. Working on this has, for me, been time with my Heavenly Father, and it has been great! My sincere hope is that you, the reader, will find things that you will take away to enhance your relationship with God. As you read, when you see something you like I encourage you to say, "I'll take that!" This is what I do when I read something that touches me.

I've included many scriptural references and quotes, all of which are my personal paraphrase. I learned many years ago that part of effective study is to put the text in your own words. It helps to remember it and can aid in gaining a deeper meaning.

I realize that if people do not read introductions, then they most likely do not read acknowledgments. With this thought in mind, I will not acknowledge anyone, but I will give some shout-outs. As I've noted in my other books, there are many others who have contributed to my thoughts and the final draft. First, this work would not have been possible without the Holy Spirit, who has guided me throughout and many times told me it was not time to stop when I thought it was. The Holy Spirit is my closest companion, and I look forward to spending eternity with Him, the Lord Jesus, and the Father. I freely confess that I am a mere vessel in the production of this work. I'm grateful to CJ, Michael, Mary, Tristan, Brandon, Kensly, JJ, Ella, Blakley, Boden, Ila Ruth, and Bristol, who are my inspiration in writing this. Next, I appreciate Debi who proofs and critiques everything I write. With all my heart, I confess that without her, my activities would have little meaning. As in other projects, I greatly appreciate the encouragement of my friend and brother in Christ, Reece Bandy. As I told him, had he opined that I missed the mark in any way, I would have scrapped the whole project. I also greatly appreciate the feedback I received from the late Brenda Lane. There are very few people to whom Debi, and I look up to and Brenda and Dr. Lane have been foremost. For over 40 years she and the late Dr. William L. Lane have been an encouragement to us. Though they now rejoice in the presence of the Lord, I can still hear their encouraging voices and know that, with many other saints, they are cheering us on as we continue in this life. Certainly, there are many others who have contributed to this work in ways that are unknown, and I am grateful to every one of you. I believe we will know the contributions of all on that day when we excitedly gather around our Father's throne. Thank you for reading this first.

Why Children?

All our children.

"You can't even get into heaven unless you're like a child." Matthew 18:3

What is it about children that makes them so special to God? Considering Jesus' words in Matthew 18:3, as paraphrased above, it's like God would prefer that we never grow up. However, since the New Testament encourages us to mature in our faith, remaining a child forever is not an option. Yet, children remain special to God, and in the New Testament, I get the impression that Jesus never missed an opportunity to bless them. In Matthew 19:14, Jesus scolded the disciples when they tried to prevent the children from coming to Him. The Lord's response was, "Get out of the children's way so they can come to me, because only those who are like them will be getting into heaven." Besides a basic innocence, what trait is God looking for in us that would make us like children? The list of childhood characteristics is extensive, but there are three that stand out to me: faith, a sense of wonder, and malleability.

Faith is the first trait associated with children. The author of Hebrews wrote, "Faith is trusting in what we are confident is coming and being convinced of the good things we are unable to see." (11:1). When we tell a child he or she must believe in Jesus to go to heaven, more times than not that child will accept it. The problem with mature and sophisticated adults is that we are all filled with preconceived ideas and influenced by others. Children easily believe in Santa Claus, while adults scoff at such naivety. The same is true when it comes to believing in the Lord. When a child says his or her prayers, we often respond, "Isn't that cute?" Yes, it is cute, but more importantly, the child is demonstrating the kind of faith that will save our souls. The efficacy of faith was dramatically illustrated in Numbers 21:6-9. When the Israelites complained about God's provision for them, the Lord sent venomous serpents into the camp, the bites from which killed some of the people. When the Israelites cried out for help, God told Moses to make a bronze serpent and lift it up on a pole. If a snake bit anyone, they could look at the bronze serpent and live. It takes some faith to accept this. Imagine you've just been bitten by a deadly serpent and told all you have to do is look at a bronze snake on a pole. Some would scoff at the idea and die in their unbelief. Having nothing to lose, I think I would stare at it for a long time! In the same way, we look to the Lord Jesus to save us from our sins. Children have the advantage of not letting doubt get in the way of their belief. I think this simple ability to believe contributes to another trait in children: a sense of wonder.

I will never forget the looks on our children's faces on Christmas mornings: wide eyes and jumps for joy as they ran to and opened their gifts. There are other times children display this quality, but in my experience, it is most evident at Christmas time. As adults, we often lose this feeling of excitement and expectation. Yet, we should have it every morning. For me, watching the sun rise and seeing the colors of the sky and the landscape produces a sense of awe. In Psalm 8, David displayed a profound sense of wonder as he considered creation and exclaimed, "Why does God even think about mankind?" (8:4). David went on to write, "Yet You have put them in charge of Your creation." (8:6). The Apostle Paul wrote that God has prepared things for those who love Him that have never entered our minds. (1 Cor. 2:9). Moreover, Paul wrote that when we are in the presence of the Lord, we will be filled with wonder and astonishment. (2 Thessalonians 1:10). John, writing in Revelation 21:21, described the New Jerusalem as having streets of gold. That's a lot to look forward to, and it lasts forever! If we trust in the Lord Jesus for our salvation, we should be like children looking forward to Christmas. God holds nothing back for His children. (Psalm 84:11). In addition to faith and wonder, children are uniquely malleable.

To be malleable means that one is teachable and moldable. This is especially true of children. I've noticed that young children often mirror their parents' mannerisms. In a sense, they are being molded into their parents' image. God is looking for those who will be molded into His image. We've all heard and used the saying, "You can't teach an old dog new tricks." From personal experience, I think this is true. Yet, when we come to our Lord Jesus, we must be willing to let the Holy Spirit change us so we can grow spiritually and let go of any ideas that hold us back. As Paul wrote in 2 Corinthians 5:17, when someone believes in Christ, that person is a new creature. As a new being, we must desire to grow spiritually. Like a child's continuous questioning, we must ask, seek, and knock on heaven's door until we comprehend things that elude us. This is what the disciples did when they did not understand the Lord's parables. They asked for an explanation. (Mark 4:10). The psalmist wrote in Psalm 53:2 that God is looking for those who are looking for Him. As we are made new creations, our desire should be to imitate God. When our children and grandchildren were young, they often wanted to dress like us and do the things we did. Just as children want to imitate their parents and grandparents, we should imitate God. The Lord Jesus said that the things He did were the things He saw the Father doing. (John 5:19). As the Lord did what God the Father did, we should, like a child, want to do what Jesus did. If we are malleable in this way, we will be "letting our lights shine before others, that they may see our good deeds and glorify our Father in heaven." (Matthew 5:16).

As I think about children, I realize we are not at all called to immaturity. We are called to believe

like a child and trust God, to always stand in awe of
what He is doing, and to allow the Holy Spirit to
transform us into His image. When we allow Him to
work in us in these ways, we are already in His
kingdom.

Meet JJ and Ella

JJ, Ella and me with Granny's new table

"Consider this; that children are God's gift to us, and a great reward." Psalm 127:3

"My Lord's tender affections will never end because his intimate concern for me will never fail. They begin anew every single day! How awesome is Your faithfulness!" Lamentations 3:22-23

Sometimes entertaining grandchildren can be a challenge for grandparents. Usually, it is a full-time job that demands all our attention. One day I was with JJ in our garage when JJ noticed a project he had begun. It was a few pieces of oddly shaped lumber he was trying to form into a table for Debi. "Hey, I need to finish making Granny's table," he said. I looked at the wood he wanted to use and remembered I had some scraps that might be just what he needed. The scraps consisted of some legs I had removed from an old table and a round piece of plywood. "Well, JJ," I said, "what about these. You can make Granny's table with this wood." JJ was quick to agree. Then Ella came out and wanted to take part in our little project. So, I essentially had five pieces of wood and two children to try and make something for Debi.

I placed the plywood on a couple of sawhorses and, using a tape measure and square, had JJ draw a square on the bottom of the plywood. Then I had him draw where the legs should go. Ella then made an x in each square so JJ would know where to drill. With the x-marks in place I had JJ drill holes in the top and then as Ella and I held the legs in place he used some wood screws to stabilize the legs. Once we had completed the little project, we turned it over and it turned out pretty good. JJ and Ella were as excited as two children could be as I carried the table to where Debi was. Before I walked through the door, Ella very excitedly proclaimed, "We have a surprise for you!" The exhilaration in her voice made my day. They had just made something for their Granny, and the results filled them with such delight that Debi and I were both overwhelmed with their love. Debi and I have learned through JJ and Ella that, as the prophet Jeremiah exclaimed in

Lamentations 3:23, our God's affection and concern for us are new every day. It's like each morning God is excitedly saying. "I have a surprise for you!" Surprise has been the operative word when it comes to our grandchildren.

I've long heard people say, "If I'd known grandchildren were this great I would have had them first." I have personally been a grandparent for over 20 years now, and since my oldest ones do not live nearby I really could not identify with other grandparents. It was always fun to be with Tristan, Brandon, and Kensley for their brief visits, but these were not sufficient to lend themselves to building deep relationships, which are based on extended time together. That all changed when our daughter, Mary, wedded.

Thankfully, she and her husband, Jerry remained in the local area near us. Debi and I were finally empty nesters, and it was great! Then, a few years later, Mary and Jerry moved in an apartment attached to our house, for nearly three years, as they were preparing to build a house of their own behind us. During this time, a wonderful thing happened; Mary gave birth to a boy! His name is Jerry Allen, Jr., but we just call him JJ (Jerry, Jr.). For my wife, Debi, it was like being a mother to an infant again as Mary went back to work and Debi took care of little JJ for the first fifteen months. As is the case with all little ones, he grew like a weed. It didn't take him long to learn to walk and begin climbing all over everything. Forget the child gates designed to keep toddlers in; JJ just climbed over them! Within a little over a year, Mary gave birth to another child, this one a girl named Ella. She, too, has grown like her brother and wants to try everything he does, at least once, but she always returns to her own interests.

Since Debi and I got to see JJ and Ella every day, I became attached to them in ways that were new to me. As other grandparents can attest to, I love them more than I thought possible. I believe the thing about being a grandparent is that you know how to avoid mistakes made with your own children. Like the late Harry Chapin sang in his song, "Cat's in the Cradle," children grow up and get away before we are ready for them to leave. The day my oldest son left home to join the Air Force, I could only say to him, "For the times you wanted to play cars and I was too busy, I'm sorry." As a grandparent, I now know to drop what I'm doing when JJ says, "Play cars with me, Dandy," or Ella says, "Let's play a game." While our children turned out well, and I don't believe Debi and I made any major mistakes, with JJ and Ella, this is now our chance to do it better. Mary, Jerry, JJ, and Ella finally moved out of the house. The great aspect of this is that they built a house right behind us, so JJ and Ella are still very close.

The amazing aspect of grand-parenting, for me, has more to do with learning about and growing in my relationship with God than anything else. With them, I'm reminded of what Jesus said in Mark 10:15, "Whoever does not accept God's kingdom as a child will not go in at all." I have spent much of my life in teaching roles, and tend to look at the world academically. Though I spent a career in the Air Force, serving in many different capacities, I actually studied for the ministry and obtained my Master's

Degree in Humanities, which consisted primarily of Biblical studies. I considered myself a serious follower of Jesus Christ and have been for many years a teacher of the Bible. What I have learned through my grandchildren, JJ and Ella is the marvel of relationship; the difference between knowing about and actually knowing. My relationship with the Lord, of over 40 years, has gone through many good times, and some I wish I could do over. However, the depth and closeness were not where they should have been, and worse, I didn't know it could be better. It has taken two rambunctious children, beginning at birth and now six and five to teach me about what I was missing.

Now, I would like to introduce you to JJ and Ella. They are both very agile, and JJ is especially fearless for a young man of his age. During a recent carnival, JJ asked me to ride one of the more challenging rides with him. I said yes, and while JJ did just fine and wanted to do it several more times, old Dandy didn't do quite as well. JJ eagerly takes on challenges other older children avoid like rock walls. As I mentioned earlier, he was climbing on everything at a very early age. Ella will try anything JJ does once, and usually says that's enough and returns to more artistic activities. JJ loves to do everything his dad, Jerry, and I do. These interests include mechanics, woodworking, marksmanship, archery, driving and whittling. Since Jerry and I are both bald, JJ even thinks he should shave his head. Ella feels this way about Mary and Debi. She wants to wear the same type clothes and engage in the same activities of her Mom and Granny. Essentially, you name it and they love to do it. JJ and Ella live about two-tenths of a mile behind us, and we frequently get calls from Mary saying they are on the way to our house. Nowadays, there are times they just show up. When Debi and I know they're coming we'll look out the window and here they come. Sometimes they will be driving up on a small four-wheeler or Ella's battery-operated jeep. Something that gives me great joy is that many times when JJ and Ella are with us, they do not want to go home; they would rather be with us. In a nutshell, that's JJ and Ella who have been so instrumental in my relationship with the greatest God who could ever be.

God speaks to each of us in many different ways. One of these ways might be an actual audience with God. In this regard, a close friend of mine actually experienced being in the physical presence of the Holy Spirit. This is an experience I wish I could have, but God has used a different method for communicating with me. I've come to learn there are two things working together in teaching me. First is my knowledge of scripture. I have not memorized the entire Bible, but I know it well and it is hidden in my heart as Psalm 119:9-11 encourages us to do. Second is the Holy Spirit Himself. In John 14:26, Jesus told the disciples that the Holy Spirit would be our teacher and bring to mind the things Jesus said. This has been my experience. The Holy Spirit speaks to me daily through scriptures in my heart and the events around me. In Maltbie Babcock's famous hymn, "This is My Father's World," there is the phrase, "He speaks to me everywhere." This has become my experience, and JJ and Ella have been a

15

big part of it. The following vignettes are the events that the Holy Spirit has used to get my attention, and I have shared them as often as I can. I sincerely hope they speak to you as they have to me, and I hope that you can hear God saying, "I have a surprise for you!"

Fearfully and Wonderfully Made and Saved

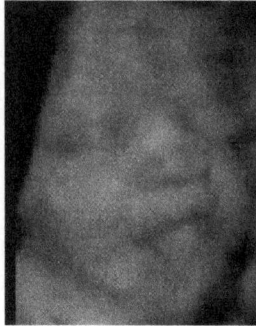

Preborn JJ

"You very carefully made me from the inside out within my mother, Wow! I cannot thank you enough because of the way You have put my body together. You do the most incredible things!" Psalm 139:13-14

"You have been rescued and restored by unmerited favor through confidence that is not even your own; it is God's gift, and not based on anything you could possibly do so that no one can arrogantly claim the credit for being right with God." Ephesians 2:8-9

Mary and Jerry had been married for five years with no children coming along. However, I was pretty sure they would have two girls very close in age based on a dream I had, in which I was on the floor playing with them. Somehow, I knew this was a prophetic dream, and looked forward to its fulfillment. Sure enough, Mary unexpectedly came up pregnant. I told her that she would have a girl, but the ultrasound proved me wrong. When our children were born we had ultrasounds that, according to the doctor showed the position of the baby and in some cases gave away the sex of the child. All the ultrasounds I saw were a garbled mess, and in each instance, every one of our children's gender was a well-kept secret until the time of delivery. Nowadays they have 3-D ultrasounds that present a very detailed image of the child. I was amazed at the detail of JJ's picture. Moreover, when he was born, he actually looked like the ultrasound picture.

I was with Debi for the births of all our children. Each one was a distinct miracle. There are so many aspects of the assembling of a preborn child, and we often take it for granted even though we do refer to it as the miracle of birth. Beginning from microscopic elements children take form and grow into incredibly complex beings with everything needed to survive in the world. As the Psalmist wrote, "we were very carefully put together from the inside out, within our mothers." As I reflected on this, I realized that there is a spiritual aspect when it comes to our salvation.

In the second chapter of Ephesians, Paul said, "You have been rescued and restored by unmerited favor through confidence that is not even your own; it is God's gift, and not based on anything you could possibly do so that no one can arrogantly claim the credit for being right with God." This is a passage of scripture that I memorized many years ago as a young believer. I think I always understood the gist of it, but as I've grown older it has taken on a deeper meaning. Just as JJ and Ella and indeed all of us, were intricately put together out of sight and without our assistance so through the sacrifice of our Lord Jesus Christ we are saved, and literally, as the Lord said, born again.

In John chapter three, the author recounts the story of Nicodemus coming to Jesus. In this encounter Nicodemus, the scholarly Pharisee, recognized that God was with Jesus based on the works He was doing. By coming to Jesus as he did Nicodemus clearly demonstrated that he wanted to know more about what God was doing at the time. Jesus responded to him in an unusual, yet direct manner by going straight to the heart of the matter. The Lord told him we must be born a second time if we want to experience the Kingdom of God. This answer completely threw Nicodemus off as he was thinking in physical/worldly terms rather than spiritual. The mistake of confusing physical and spiritual is like mixing apples and oranges; it just doesn't work; it's like putting new wine into old wineskins. Jesus went on to explain that we must have a spiritual rebirth and that the physical world is not equipped to understand matters of this nature.

To appreciate why we must move from a flesh existence to a spiritual one consider the world around us; it gets old and decays. I have an old family picture of my grandmother and her siblings when she was a young girl. Of course, I never saw her as a young woman, but through pictures taken over the years I can see the progression from youth to old age and eventual death. In fact, I notice it every time I look in the mirror! We all grow old and die. We often want to think of our future heavenly existence as being much like the world as we know it, only better. However, it has to be different because there will be no death and decay in God's Kingdom. As Paul said in First Corinthians 15:50, "our fleshly bodies cannot enter the Kingdom of God." What is spirit does not decay or grow old, so when we are born again, our spirits are ready for this experience of eternal freshness. Thus, the question becomes how does this rebirth take place?

Jesus told Nicodemus that whoever believes and has faith, in Him has eternal life. In this regard, John 1:12 opens his gospel saying, "Yet for all who did accept Him, He gave the benefit of being God's children, to include those who have faith in His name." Hebrews 11:1 defines faith as the "confidence of receiving things anticipated and being persuaded that there is another world that is unseen." Consequently, our faith in Jesus Christ means that we are convinced He is able to, as Jude 24 says, "bring us confidently, without blemish into His glorious presence with elation beyond our imaginations."

The real wonder of it all is what Jesus did to bring us to this point-He sacrificed His life in the most brutal fashion imaginable. As I mentioned earlier, I was with Debi for the births of every one of our children, so I have an inkling of an idea of what mothers go through in childbirth. In a way that was significantly greater, our Lord Jesus Christ endured incredible pain to bring us to this point. In fact, in John 16:21, Jesus compared what He was about to endure with childbirth, essentially saying that once the child is born she [the mother] forgets the pain because of the joy associated with the newborn child. We are those children!

When Jesus spoke with Nicodemus in John 3:16, he spoke those wonderful words, "God loves the lost people in the world so much He was willing to sacrifice His only Son born into the world that whoever has confidence in Him will not pass away, but rather have life that never ends." John went on to add in 1 John 4:10, "Now this is love, not that we loved God, but He loved us first and sent His one and only Son to pay the full price for our sins." The common theme throughout the New Testament is that God loves us that much! Through our Lord Jesus Christ, no matter what happens, we now have life that never ends. He has fearfully and wonderfully saved us!

A Sloppy Wet Kiss

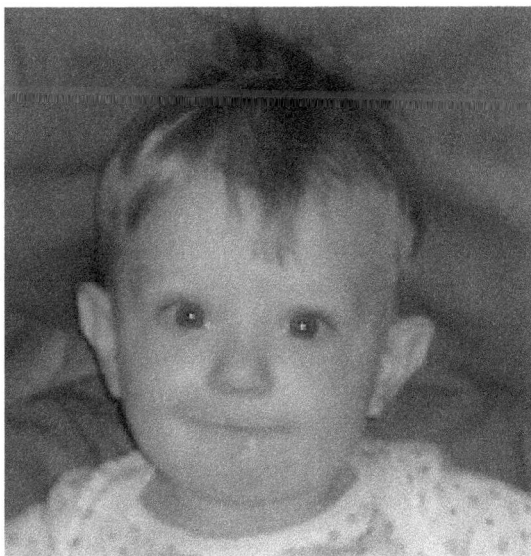

"I have nothing in heaven but You, and in this world, there is nothing I want more than You."
Psalm 73:25

A great joy for Debi and me is getting a big hug from JJ and Ella before they leave to go home. I remember one day, in particular, JJ had been with us and was about to leave with Mary and Jerry. As usual, I picked the little guy up and said, "Give me a big hug!" Immediately he responded with what we refer to as a "hulker hug," and followed it up with, an unexpected, very sloppy, and very wet kiss right on the lips! No sooner had he done this than I very distinctly sensed the Lord say, "This is what I want from you."

So, I ask, how do we give God All Mighty, creator, and sustainer of all things, a big kiss? Given this particular question and based on dictionary definitions, a kiss as an expression of fondness, adoration, as a salutation, or as a sign of admiration, or worship. Wow, now this is beginning to make sense! All of these terms can be summed up in one word, and that is worship. Throughout the scriptures, we are called to worship the Lord. In the earliest use of this term in Genesis 22:5, as Abraham is about to ascend the mountain to sacrifice his son Isaac, he says "we will go worship." In this case, worship involved sacrifice, initially Abraham thought he would have to sacrifice his son, but thankfully the Lord's angel prevented him from doing so and provided a ram instead. According to this story, God was interested to see what Abraham was willing to sacrifice for Him, which was his promised son. Of course in our culture, we do not offer ritualistic sacrifices, but I've learned over the years there is something our Heavenly Father still desires from us and that is the sacrifice of praise.

Psalm 100:4 says to "come into His courts with praise." In the Bible, the number of references to praising God is incredible, especially in the Psalms. The word praise means to show your approval or admiration for someone or something. Generally, when we think of this word something else comes to mind which is excitement. I consider myself to be an aficionado of hot sauces. Every now and then I find something that I get really excited about and let all my fellow enthusiasts know about my new culinary find. The same can be said for

23

movies we enjoy, sports teams we follow, and most anything you can think of. Since this is a book about my grandchildren, you might guess that I go overboard when it comes to what my boys and girls can do. We are a world full of praise. Yet, how much praise is God receiving from our lips?

Jeremiah 9:23-24 says, "Hear what the Lord says, "I don't want to hear a wise person brag about being wise, I don't want to hear a strong person proudly crow about their strength, and I don't want to hear a rich person vaunt about all their money. But this is what I do want to hear, boasting that a person has a personal relationship with Me, and comprehends My ways, that I am the Lord of all creation and that I exercise loving-kindness, justice, and righteousness throughout the world because these are the things I take pleasure in says the Lord."" In church settings, I frequently hear congregates utter, "Praise the Lord!" I do believe in every instance these are sincere expressions of worship. However, I get the impression we are not going near far enough in our giving of praise.

As Jeremiah said, our God wants us to boast about our relationship with Him. The Apostle Paul made this clear in First Corinthians 1:31, and Second Corinthians 10:17, as he said, "whoever is going to boast let that person boast in the Lord." In this regard, as Paul said in Philippians 3:7-11, he considered his worldly accomplishments as less than rubbish compared to knowing the Lord Jesus Christ. Jesus also touched on this in Matthew 13:44-46, when He compared the Kingdom of Heaven to the pearl of great price, and the treasure found hidden in a field, both of which were worth all a person had that he or she might acquire them.

Another, more visual, example of giving God the praise He deserves from us is the description provided in Second Samuel 6:14-16 of King David dancing before the Lord with all his might as the Ark of the Covenant is brought into Jerusalem. In this instance, David's princess bride, Michal the daughter of King Saul, saw David's rejoicing and dancing before the Lord, and as the scriptures say, "despised him in her heart." According to this passage, Michal considered David's dancing was undignified for a king. Yet David was undeterred in his love and devotion for God, replying to Michal that he would continue to humble himself before the Lord. As I have meditated on JJ's kiss and King David's dancing before the Lord, I have to conclude that this is the best example I can find of giving to God what He desires from us-a sloppy wet kiss.

The bottom line to all this is that our relationship with God through our Lord Jesus is more valuable than anything the world has to offer or anything that we might have. Thus, like King David, we should be making a big deal about what our God is to us. So, if you want to give God a big, sloppy wet kiss like JJ did to me, don't be shy; brag about Him!

Sleeping in My Lap

"In perfect peace I can lie down and sleep soundly because You, Lord, are my security."
Psalm 4:8

"Stop struggling and recognize that I am God Almighty. I will be highly exalted among all nations and My magnificent glory will cover the earth."
Psalm 46:10

There are few things more meaningful to me than having my grandchildren sit in my lap and fall asleep. Unfortunately, as they grow older, like their parents, my children before them, they are less willing to fall asleep on my lap. However, in the first few years of JJ's and Ella's lives, this was a daily occurrence. I had retired from my second career and was home to help Debi take care of our two little "munchkins." The routine was to eat lunch then put on some soft music and let the children fall asleep.

From the beginning, JJ was resistant to taking a nap, much like his grandfather before him. Still, I loved holding him and having him fall asleep while in my lap. Even now, as he is older (6 years old), I still love grabbing those now rare moments of this kind of closeness. So, it occurred to me that if I loved this kind of closeness with JJ, how much more does my Father in Heaven desire alone time with me?

I'm not sure if it has to do with age, or recognition of the times in which we live, or perhaps a combination of the two, but I'm increasingly aware of the need for prayer, one-on-one time with God. An aspect of this recognition is noticing how much time Jesus spent in prayer. Throughout the Gospels, Jesus is depicted as going alone to a mountain for prayer, sometimes after sending his disciples on to their next destination. I think this is instructive to us. If Jesus, being God incarnate, needed to spend time in prayer with God the Father, how much more do we need to do this? And yet, we, most of us, spend very little time in prayer. Prayer is a privilege that all of us take so much for granted and thereby completely miss what is available to us.

There is so much more to prayer than asking for things because, at its heart, prayer is about relationship. For most of us, we do not have access to the high and mighty of this world. In most cases, even if we did have free access to people of power, the President of the United States, for example, we would not just run into the office on a whim. However, with the God of the universe, who is beyond our comprehension in power and authority, through Jesus Christ our redeemer, we do have this kind of entrance. There is a story that has touched me about the Austro-Hungarian Archduke Ferdinand and his children. He is said to have loved his children so much that, even when he was entertaining guests, when his children came to him, he would stop what he was doing and play with them on the floor.

I believe this story of Archduke Ferdinand is meaningful to me because it is a concrete example of the way our Heavenly Father feels about us. In verse 4:16, the writer of Hebrews said that because Jesus, our high priest, has gone before us, "we can come boldly to the throne of grace to find mercy and grace in time of need." Yet, we don't have to wait until there is a need to enter in. As Jesus told the woman at the well in John 4:23, the Father seeks people who will worship Him in spirit and in truth. Our Heavenly Father wants us to call out to Him, spend time with Him, and learn from Him. As God said through the prophet in Jeremiah 33:3, He wants us to call to Him and seek Him so that He can tell us things, "secrets," we do not know. In fact, Psalm 25:14 says as much: "God shares his secrets with those who stand in reverent awe of Him."

If we do not spend time with the Father, or only a few minutes each day, then when do we have the opportunity to hear what He wants to tell us? As a retired military officer and now retired teacher, I have learned many things that only life experiences can provide that I can share with my children and grandchildren. Yet, if my children and grandchildren never take the time to sit with me and ask about these experiences, they will not gain the benefit that may be there, even though it was available to them all the time. Not only is there the opportunity to grow in our spiritual insights, rest is another aspect of the relationship.

Biblically, we are all called to enter God's rest. In fact, this is what Jesus said in Matthew 11:28, when He essentially says, "Everyone who is tired and worn out from toil, come to Me and I will give you rest." The writer of Hebrews also speaks of entering God's rest. The rest the author of Hebrews refers to is through believing in the Lord Jesus Christ. When we believe, He becomes our righteousness and salvation so that we no longer have to toil in vain to gain God's acceptance! For JJ and Ella, all they had to do was to be born to gain my acceptance. For this reason, they may sit in my lap anytime they want, and I actually long for them to do so. Even when I am busy with other things, I love to take time for them to sit with me.

Once, when their mother, Mary, was about 9 years old, she walked into my study one evening while I was working. When I looked up, she said, with a long face, "I'm not having a very good day." At this, I stopped what I was doing, had her sit in my lap, and asked her to tell me about it. Would you believe we have this privilege with God? The Apostle Peter, in First Peter 5:7, wrote that we are to "cast all our worries upon Him because He cares for us." He really does! Just as I would not turn away my daughter, I will not turn away my grandchildren because I care about them. In the very same way, our Heavenly Father feels the same for each of us.

You may wonder why God wants us in such a relationship. That He wants us to spend time with

Him really is amazing grace. I believe that from the beginning, God created mankind to be in a relationship with Him, unlike any other created being. I think Genesis 3:8-9 holds a message for us in this regard. This passage notes that God was walking in the garden in the cool of the day, and calling for Adam and Eve. The thought that comes to me is that this was probably a routine meeting between God and the two He had created in His image. In other words, this was an essential part of the relationship. Genesis 5:22-24 picks up on the thought of relationship as it records Enoch walking with God for 300 years. Suddenly, it states that Enoch disappeared because God took him. I heard a pastor describe the passage in this way: "Enoch was walking so close to God that the Lord said, "Since you're this close, come on up all the way!"" Though the Bible contains many examples of personal relationships with God, there is one, in particular, that should encourage all of us-David.

King David is described as a "man after God's own heart." While David did some mighty acts of faith, such as slaying the giant Goliath, he was also very fallible and did things that we would hardly expect from anyone said to be "after God's own heart." The key to understanding David is to realize that he never stopped seeking God. In Second Samuel 12, when confronted regarding his sin with Bathsheba and the murder of her husband, Uriah, David's response was, "I have sinned." He did not make excuses, and he did not give up by saying, "I'll never be good enough." David placed himself in God's hands and looked to Him for mercy. Psalm 51 details David's prayer at this time as he looks to God's mercy, compassion, and ability to erase his sin. The lesson is not that we should willingly sin with the expectation of instant forgiveness, but that our heavenly Father is not looking for perfect sons and daughters, but rather those who never stop getting up after they stumble.

We have a tendency to think of these examples, along with all the heroes of faith, as exceptions to the rule, but I believe they are the rule and the rest of us are missing out on something incredible. It is important for us to understand that, through Jesus Christ, God has already done everything needed for each of us to enjoy a relationship with Him as close as any Biblical person of faith! It will be no surprise to say that my little JJ, from time to time, gets into some kind of trouble. He is at that age where he does some limit testing, and from time to time, Debi and I have to correct him. Even when JJ deliberately does something against my wishes, there is never a time I do not want him to come and be with me. Much like the father depicted in the story of the prodigal son, who watched for his son's return and saw him from a distance and ran to him, I watch for JJ and Ella, and our Father in Heaven watches for us. For our part, we should as Paul admonished in First Thessalonians 5:17, "never stop praying." Like Archduke Ferdinand, and the prodigal's father, God longs to be with us, and our response should be that we long to be with Him.

I want to end this chapter with one final thought about the brother of the prodigal son. This is the brother who faithfully worked for his father day in and day out and never took the time to enjoy what he had. As you will recall, following the prodigal's return, his brother was walking in from the field and heard the celebration. Rather than go in and join the festivity, the father had to go out to him. When the faithful son protested that he never had a party, but his faithless brother was getting one, the father replied that everything was his and he could have celebrated at any time. Jesus told the story of the prodigal son to illustrate his comment recorded in Luke 15:10 that the angels in heaven rejoice whenever a soul is saved. The lesson for us is that everything is there for us as children of God to live a life of continuous celebration. There is no need to be like the faithful son, who forgot the relationship he could have had with his father. With this in mind, we should all spend more time in our Father's lap.

All This is Ours

JJ taking over my desk.

"Everything belongs to you." First Corinthians 3:21

"We don't focus on the visible world; our focus is on the invisible realm because the things that are seen are transitory while the things that are not seen are eternal." Second Corinthians 4:18

We live in a world in which status is many times determined by wealth and possessions. Even though we are often quick to repeat the well-known phrase, "money isn't everything," in reality, we live as if it were. So many times, we define ourselves by the work we do, the money we make, the clothes we wear, the house we live in, and the vehicle we drive. Of all these things listed, none will survive past our brief lifetimes. For this reason, Paul correctly told the Corinthian Church in Second Corinthians 4:18 to look beyond the transitory to what is permanent.

When it comes to transitory possessions, my home study is filled with memorabilia from 40 years of adventurous work, much of which spanned the globe. Books, knick-knacks, swords, and pictures cover the walls and are enough to capture the imagination of any young child like JJ. One afternoon, while JJ was napping, I slipped out and went to my study to do some work. Upon waking up, if I was not in the room, JJ always asked Debi, "Where's Dandy?" Debi would reply, "Dandy is in his office." On this particular day, JJ came in still sleepy-eyed and sat in my lap. These times were among those very special moments of being together. After slumping down for a moment, he sat up and looked about the study as if he had just noticed all the things around him. JJ then looked up at me, and, while thoughtfully nodding his head, said, "All this is our stuff." My reply was, "Yes, this is all our stuff." As my grandson, he is an heir to all my earthly possessions, and I take pleasure in telling him they will be his, though he does have to share with his cousin Brandon. But the larger lesson has to do with what is ours through our Heavenly Father. In fact, because of JJ's comment, I've come to the point that when I look up at the stars in the sky, I like to say, "All this is our stuff, Father."

The old nursery rhyme, "twinkle twinkle little star," contains more truth than you might expect when it describes stars "like a diamond in the sky." Astronomers have come to realize that there are huge planets and former stars that are literally enormous diamonds floating in space. Moreover, I recently read that astronomers have discovered a distant planet that rains rubies and sapphires. Based on these discoveries, the thought that comes to mind is that the things we consider most valuable are as common as the sand on the seashore in our universe. While we have yet to discover a planet made entirely of gold, it would not surprise me if someday scientists discovered one. Discoveries of this nature add additional meaning to John's description of the New Jerusalem, adorned with gold and precious stones, in Revelation 21:10-27. Thus, the inheritance we have to look forward to is far beyond our ability to comprehend.

In John 14:2-3, Jesus said that in His Father's house are many mansions and that He was going to prepare a place for us. Whenever I read this, I can't help but think about these recent astronomical discoveries. Besides precious stones in space, thanks to the Hubble Space Telescope and other space-based devices, we are able to view sights that people could not imagine from the beginning of mankind to recent times. Looking through these instruments, astronomers have estimated there are one hundred billion galaxies in the universe. It occurred to me that if there are so many galaxies, our Father could easily give each of us our own galaxy! I suppose that each of these galaxies could be complete with planets and stars of precious materials. Thinking about it this way makes the planet we live on ever so small. If we are as special as the Bible tells us, "created in God's image,…a little lower than God," (Genesis 1:26-27; Psalm 8:5) then forget the sky, there is no limit!

In the first two chapters of Genesis, God created the world, within which was a special garden. After creating the animals, He then created mankind and essentially gave everything over to Adam and Eve. In Genesis 1:28, He said, "Have lots of children, enough to fill the world. Make the world, and everything in it your own, and be kings and queens over it." What a gift! God gave them everything! Still, I can't help thinking that the greatest gift was their close relationship with God. Imagine every evening God walking up to you and saying, "Tell me about your day." This incredible gift did come with the condition that they obey God's instructions. Unfortunately, they lost it when they gave into temptation, but here we do get a first glimpse of what our Father wants to give us.

We get another glimpse of this in Genesis 15:1, when God said to Abraham, "I am your shield and your very great reward." There are many different translations of this particular verse, but to me, the thought that God Himself is our reward has always stuck with me. This is supported in the Psalms as Psalm 16:5, which says, "The Lord is my inheritance," and then again, Psalm 73:26 says, "God is my fortitude and my everlasting portion." While there are many other references throughout scripture to support the thought that God Himself is ours to treasure forever, these passages give you the idea. In Song of Solomon 6:3, the author wrote, "I belong to my lover and my lover belongs to me." This is a particularly meaningful verse as it not only applies to an intimate marital relationship on Earth; it also applies to our relationship with God. He is our God, and He belongs to us in this relationship as we belong to Him. The Old Testament reinforces this imagery as the prophets refer to Israel as a wayward wife, e.g., Hosea, and Ezekiel 23, and the New Testament continues this description as it refers to the Church as the "Bride of Christ." (Revelation 19:6-8).

If we are married to God, then what belongs to us? The answer is everything that belongs to God is ours. Many marriages today begin with prenuptial agreements to prevent either the bride or the groom from losing wealth in a divorce. However, when Debi and I married while we were in college, I had never heard of such a thing, and I entered the marriage with the thought that what was mine was hers and what was hers was mine. For nearly fifty years, this has been the case for us. Still, my focus has never been on anything of value that Debi brought to the marriage, but solely on her and our relationship. I'm confident that this is also her focus as well. So it is with us in our relationship with God. While we are heirs to untold wealth, the real treasure is our God, and Father who loved us so much He redeemed us through His Son, Jesus Christ.

In Jeremiah 9:23-24, God says, "Listen to Me, "I don't want the wise person bragging about his or her wisdom, and I don't want to hear a bragging about their strength, and I really don't want to hear of some wealthy person boasting of how rich they are; but what I do want to hear is that he or she understands and knows Me, that I am Lord over all, and that I ordain mercy, justice, and righteousness throughout the world because I love these things.'"

Thus, the most important thing to our Father is that we not just know about Him, but intimately know Him, and how He works. Someone once asked Albert Einstein's Wife if she understood his work. Her answer was, "No, but I understand Dr. Einstein." There are many things that we cannot understand regarding the work our Father has done and how He will achieve His purpose. However, like Mrs. Einstein, we can understand our God.

In my experience, the closer I get to the Father, the closer I want to get. I have never obtained any possession that retained its ability to satisfy. Fashions change, I gain weight, cars get old, gadgets break down, and so it goes. Only my relationship with God and spending time with Him, whether on my knees or praying throughout the day fills that empty spot. Even though I can look up at the stars in the sky and confidently say, "All this is ours, Father," I do not identify myself based on what I will have, but rather based on knowing and understanding Him.

Eating off My Plate

Our charming grandchildren.

"And God rained heavenly bread down on them so they would have food. The very food of heaven He sent to them in great abundance." Psalm 78:24-25

"He eagerly calls me to His great feast, and He has covered me with His love."
Song of Solomon 2:4

I will never forget the first time JJ walked in and grabbed a piece of food off my plate. For the first two years of JJ's life, Mary and Jerry were living in an apartment attached to our home. It was not uncommon for them to walk in at any time. Debi and I frequently watch the news as we eat our dinner. On this particular occasion, I can't remember exactly what I was eating, but I know it was a finger food. As the young family walked in to see what we were doing, before I could turn around, JJ walked by and casually took a piece of food off my plate and began eating it. I was impressed by how natural this came to him and it warmed my heart to have a little man who was comfortable enjoying what I was eating. In the few years since that time, it is almost a daily occurrence to hear either JJ or Ella, say, "I'm hungry." It is also very common for Debi and me to find something we know they enjoy. The act of eating someone's food is a good sign of closeness.

As a young single man, a roommate and I lived in an apartment in Philadelphia for a couple of years. My roommate and I had an assortment of friends and colleagues who would come over to visit. Those who knew us best, and were comfortable being with us, would come in and open our refrigerator to see what we might have to eat. I can assure you that back in those days the pickings were few. Yet the point remains that we can be comfortable visiting in someone's home, but looking through their refrigerator is a whole new dimension of relationship. This is the kind of thing I feel comfortable doing at my parents' home, but really there are no other places where I would be at ease with such an act. In the case of JJ and Ella, they are both right at home checking out our refrigerator and pantry. If they can't reach the desired item, a chair is always useful for getting at it. For me, this raises the question; how much do I really feel at home in God's presence?

Before anyone can adequately answer that question, we need to have a better grasp of God's character and what He expects. In the Old Testament, God was very severe with his people. Two examples come readily to mind here. First is the death of

Aaron's sons, Nadab and Abihu. In this event recorded in Leviticus 10:1-2, the two brothers offered the Lord incense using fire that was not authorized, and fire from the presence of the Lord struck them dead. The second example is from Second Samuel 6:6-7 when Uzzah died for touching the Ark of the Covenant. In this instance, God had given the Israelites specific instructions as to how they were to transport the Ark. Four priests were to carry it on their shoulders using the supporting rods made with it. However, when King David transported the Ark to Jerusalem the priests were transporting it on an ox-drawn cart. When the oxen stumbled and made the Ark unstable, Uzzah reached out to steady the symbol of God's presence to keep it from falling off the cart. While to us this may seem to be a responsible act, Uzzah was struck dead for touching the sacred object. The great lesson in both these instances is when God gives you specific instructions, follow them to the letter! Based on these examples I would not be comfortable looking in God's refrigerator-would you? However, in the New Testament. we seem to see another, seemingly contradictory, aspect of the All Mighty.

Jesus, God incarnate, demonstrated incredible compassion during His time on earth. Throughout the New Testament, we see him healing the sick, raising the dead, feeding the hungry and teaching the poor. The only class of people with whom He clashed was the religious establishment. Even in these clashes, His goal was to free people from religious oppression. So how do we reconcile the God of the Old Testament with the Lord Jesus

41

Christ? I believe the answer is to be found in the second chapter of Hebrews. Here the author notes in verses two and three, "If the instructions spoken through angels was unchangeable, and any miss-step and noncompliance received an impartial penalty, how can we now ever get away with it if we ignore the great salvation God has now provided." The gist of this is that Jesus Christ is the new covenant; accepting His sacrifice for our sins and being clothed in the righteousness that only He can provide. If we reject this, then the penalty will be as severe as that recorded in the Old Testament. I will also note that Paul, in First Corinthians 10:11, made the point that everything recorded in the Old Testament was to provide an example for us. The bottom line is that God has not changed, but through our Lord Jesus Christ it is now so much easier to come into His presence and enjoy the wonderful things He has made available to us, which brings us back to JJ and Ella.

Because JJ's and Ella's mother is our daughter they are our grandchildren and welcome to any good thing we may have. Similarly, because we are clothed in Jesus Christ's righteousness we can go boldly into God's presence and take part in all that He has to offer, which is, by the way, unlimited! This is the reason the author of Hebrews wrote in verse 4:16, "Let's come confidently closer to the throne of unmerited favor so we can receive kindness and grace to help us when we need it." Those who have taken this to heart and earnestly seek to be in God's presence enjoy a higher level of relationship and spiritual nourishment. Physical food and spiritual food are similar in that they provide nourishment, but physical food is for the body while spiritual food is for our souls. As Jesus answered Satan in Matthew 4:4, "The scriptures say man cannot live only on bread but on God's every utterance."

Many people seem to think of the Bible as a collection of ancient writings few people can understand. However, except for some of the more esoteric passages of the Old Testament, it is remarkably straightforward and provides God's guidance for living in a way that is pleasing to Him. Moreover, as a person studies the scriptures, he or she will become more aware of God's thoughts. Of course, the conclusion is that the more we know of God's thoughts the more intimate we become with Him.

Our Heavenly Father has a spiritual refrigerator that is stocked full just for us. I am convinced that He eagerly watches for His children to come in, open the door, and grab something. Each time we pick up the Bible and learn something new, it is like JJ walking by and taking food off my plate or he and Ella looking through the refrigerator. Since God is unlimited, He is not worried about running out of anything. The worst thing we can do is ignore what He has to offer. So, I encourage you to go in and grab as much as you can.

The Specialness of Being Close

Ella and JJ enjoying the rainbow with Ruby our dog looking on.

"The Lord has a close relationship to everyone who takes the time to look for Him, and sincerely seek to be in His presence." Psalm 145:18

I was praying one morning and as I gave thanks for all my children and grandchildren, I gave special thanks for JJ and Ella. During this prayer time, I mentioned that they were special because they were close. The moment I mentioned this I sensed the Holy Spirit say, "Funny how that works." Point well made! It is not a matter of the ones closest to us being a little more special, it is all about a deeper relationship that develops based on time spent together. Wow! If I feel closer to JJ and Ella because of the extra time we have together, how much more is this the case in our relationship to our Heavenly Father?

The God of the universe, our Heavenly Father wants to have a close and thriving relationship with every human being. A cursory reading of the scriptures might give one the impression that the All Mighty is in heaven picking and choosing those he wants to bring near. In fact, He appears quite harsh, when you consider passages like Malachi 1:2-3, "I loved Jacob, but I hated Esau." We can also go all the way back to the beginning when Cain and Abel offered their sacrifices to God. In Genesis chapter four it says that when the brothers brought their sacrifices to God, He was pleased with Abel's offering but not Cain's. While passages like these do seem hard, there are many more to prove otherwise. Ezekiel 18:23 makes it clear that God is not pleased with the death of those who live wicked lives, and would rather they turn to Him. Similarly, Second Peter 3:9, refers to the Lord as being patient, not willing that any should be lost. Another passage that is special to me is First John 2:2, which says that Jesus paid the price for the sins of the whole world. Our Lord and Savior cleared the way for everybody! It all has to do with who will seek to come close to God. In the case of Cain, before he murdered his brother, God spoke to him and gently told him what he needed to do. As we know, Cain rejected that instruction.

Proverbs chapter eight is a good example of God reaching out to everyone as it portrays Lady Wisdom calling out to all who will hear and inviting them into her house for the enjoyment of what she has to offer. It seems that curiosity is a good starting point. In Exodus chapter three, Moses noticed the burning bush, and he watched it long enough to notice that though it burned, it was not reduced to ashes by the fire. Because he came closer to see what was happening, Moses had his first encounter with God. Many others would have glanced at the flaming bush, perhaps think that it was an interesting sight, and continue on their way. Moses, however, wanted to know more. This holds true for the disciples in Mark chapter four. After Jesus told the crowd the parable of the Sower, most of the crowd walked away, maybe wondering what it all meant. The disciples were different from the multitude. They were not satisfied and came to Jesus asking exactly what the parable represented. Jesus replied to them that they would receive the interpretation while the others would only hear the parable. The big difference is that the disciples had an inquiring mind. They asked and as a consequence received!

Our Heavenly Father wants every one of us to be close to Him and to ask these kinds of questions. In Jeremiah 33:3, God told the prophet, "If you will ask Me, I will answer you, and tell you the most wonderful things that you do not know." The Apostle Paul noted in First Corinthians 1:12, "We have not the spirit of this present world, but the Spirit who is from God, so we can know of the wonderful gifts He has so generously given us." As we spend time seeking God through studying the scriptures and sincere prayer, the Holy Spirit will reveal new things to us. Just like pursuing our relationship with God, because JJ spends more time with me, he gets answers to many questions. He also gets many prizes. Whenever I am working in my office, it is not uncommon for JJ to look through my desk drawers. Like most desks, there are many items that I have collected over the years and really have no use for. So, when JJ finds something, he finds interesting, he will ask, "What's this?" which really means, "May I have it?" to which I frequently reply, "You may have it." I love to give gifts to all my children and grandchildren, but because JJ and Ella are the closest and spend the most time with us, well, they get the most. Those who spend the most time with the Lord likewise get the most.

The Psalmist, in 65:4, wrote, "Those You choose to bring near to Yourself in your house have got to be the happiest people in the world. The goodness of Your dwelling place will satisfy us." It is as easy as making up your mind that you want to be close to God. James wrote in 4:8, "Come close to God and He will come close to you." I can't think of anything that would make me happier than to know I have a close relationship with God. The prophet Azariah told Judah's King Asa, in Second Chronicles 15:2, "The Lord is going to be with you as long as you are with Him. And if you go looking for Him He will let you find Him, but be warned if you go your own way and forget about God, He will let you go." Again, it is our choice as to whether or not we want to seek and find God, and whether we want to remain with Him. Moreover, the amazing thing is that if you have wondered away, you can come back!

Though I've already discussed the prodigal son it is worth mentioning again. While the son was away, his father never stopped caring for him. Any suffering the son was going through at the time was because of his own actions. I think it is important that we all understand that like the prodigal in this story, we all have to live with our own decisions, and like the father, God allows us to go our own way. There are several passages of scripture that demonstrates how our Father feels about those who have either wandered away or are lost. Zechariah 1:5 and Malachi 3:7 say essentially the same thing, "The Lord of all the angels says, "Come back to Me so that I can come back to you."" It is incredible that such an awesome God is willing to stoop down and call to those who have rejected Him. Because He never stops caring, we are all special to Him. Still, because of the basics of relationship building, spending time together, the ones who take the time to be with Him regularly will always be the closest. Just like JJ and Ella, they have a unique relationship to Debi and me because they are the closest.

The Little Red Truck

*"The Lord our God shines on us and protects us;
our Master gives us unmerited favor and splendor;
Our God does not keep back any good thing from
those who walk in His ways."*
Psalm 84:11

*"Lion cubs go without food and get hungry, but
those who follow the Lord God will not lack for any
good thing."* Psalm 34:10

*"Similarly, I want you to know that all of heaven is
joyous and excited over every single person who
turns from their sins and seeks God."* Luke 15:10

      It seemed like from the very beginning of JJ's
life he loved cars and trucks. Much like his Uncle CJ
(our oldest son) before him, there was nothing that
would excite him more than a new Hot Wheels or
Matchbox toy. Because JJ was the first grandchild on

Jerry's side of the family and Debi and I were able to spend time with him daily, miniature vehicles seemed to literally rain on our boy. In fact, he had such a huge collection it seemed unlikely that he could possibly ever miss one if he should lose it However, I was soon to learn that this was not the case.

There was one particular red truck to which JJ was attached, and he took it with him wherever he went. When JJ was about two years old, we took him, with the red truck in tow, to church one Sunday. None of us noticed when we picked him up in the nursery that he had left his truck there in the children's play area. The next few Sundays I realized that his truck was in the nursery, and it got my attention that he did too. However, I was not comfortable taking the truck as it had been there for a few weeks and I didn't want anyone to think that I was taking church property.

This went on for some time, and I believed that JJ would forget about the truck. He didn't. It had probably been a year, and JJ still mentioned the truck when we were at church. My first thought was that we could find another truck like it as a replacement, but none of us could find another truck like it anywhere. JJ was so attached to this one truck I decided to make a trip to the toy department and purchased two toy vehicles, both of greater value than the truck itself, and exchanged them for JJ's little red truck. JJ's expression upon seeing his little red truck on his toy shelf was one of those things I will never forget. He had it back and as much as a child is able, he was thankful for it.

As in every encounter with JJ, I could not help thinking that there was a meaning in this that I needed to grab ahold of. So, if I, being an imperfect grandfather, was willing to pay far more than I should for something my grandson already owned, to make him happy; what does this say about our Heavenly Father? The first thing that comes to mind is the price that our God paid to rescue us from our shortcomings. God's gift to us is a subject upon which we cannot spend too much time. As Paul noted in Romans 5:7-8, "Someone would hardly give up his or her life for a person who has lived worthily; though it is possible someone might be willing to die for someone who was a good person. Yet God clearly shows His great love for us through Christ who gave up His life for us while we were still without merit." What this passage says to me is that, in human terms, I am not worth the effort. However, John wrote, in his first epistle, that Jesus Christ died for the sins of the whole world, which includes me too. Evidently, each one of us means so much to our Heavenly Father that He was willing to do this.

There has long been a debate on the value of human life. Many believe there is no equivalent dollar value for a life. I agree with this, but our value goes far beyond what we consider to be worldly wealth. Based on our Father's actions in Jesus Christ we can only calculate the value of every one of us if we can quantify God. Personally, I don't believe this is possible. Every soul for whom our Lord died is worth more than the universe. Let that sink in! Like JJ's truck, it belonged to him, but I bought it back so he could have it again. This is what our Lord did for us. He bought us back with His own life! Yet in this story, there is another lesson for me. With all the cars and trucks JJ possessed, he never forgot about the one that was missing.

As a military member who moved frequently, I have some experience with missing items. All military families have stories of their worst moves, some of which defy the imagination. All in all, Debi and I got off easily as our worst move involved several missing boxes that no one could locate. The interesting thing about this is that we did not know what was in the lost cartons. Even more noticeable about this experience is that, aside from a couple of books I could not find, there has never been a time since that we needed whatever was in those boxes. This tells me that many of us have so much in our lives that we would not notice the absence of some of these things. This is not the case with our God-He keeps an accurate accounting of every single item!

In Matthew 6:26-30, Jesus spoke of how our Father knows the status of the birds of the air and that He took special care in decorating transitory flowers. He also went on to say that we are worth far more than these creations. The Psalmist wrote of it this way in Psalm 139:17-18, "How wonderful is Your constant attention toward me, my God! How exceedingly great are the number of your thoughts about me! If I could possibly count them the number would be greater than the grains of sand." Our Father never stops thinking about us! We are that valuable to Him, and like the father of the prodigal son, He eagerly watches for us to come to Him. This applies to every person on earth regardless of their station in life.

JJ's little red truck is so instructive and encouraging to me. Like that truck, each one of us is worth far more than you can imagine to God who paid to have us back to be His own. Also, like JJ who never forgot about that truck; our wonderful Father never forgets about us. If you ever doubt your personal worth, I encourage you to remember what God paid for you.

Watching JJ and Ella Play

"You do know that you can buy two sparrows for next to nothing, don't you? Yet I can assure you that your Father in Heaven is fully aware when one falls from the sky. Your Father in Heaven also knows how many hairs are on your head. So don't worry about anything because you are a lot more valuable than sparrows." Matthew 10:29-31

"You, Lord carefully watch all that I do, and You are intimately familiar with every tendency I have." Psalm 139:3

There have been many times that JJ and Ella have been over, and I have been able to watch them play. JJ generally wants to play with his cars and trucks. Sometimes he builds a tower so he can knock it down. Ella is the artist, always drawing pictures and giving them to Debi and me as gifts. Debi is an artist, and I like to believe I have some creative talents, so we both love to watch what our grandchildren will do with the resources they have available, and we love to see continuous improvements in the results of their play. Much of the time, we just like watching them, no matter what they are doing. I first experienced this years ago with my firstborn grandson, Brandon, who was visiting from his home in Alabama. As he was engaged in an activity I found myself thinking with admiration, "That is a smart and good looking young man." So, if I look with admiration on my children and grandchildren, how much more does our Heavenly Father look down on us and say, "That's my boy/girl!"

If we look back to the Genesis account, it is evident that as human beings created in God's image we have responsibilities. Genesis 2:19 says, "Using clay from the ground, the Lord God created and gave life to every animal of the field, forest, and sky, and presented them to Adam to see what he would call them, and whatever Adam said, that was the animal's name." From this verse, it seems that God graciously gave Adam a role in creation, and I suspect, like a proud parent, the Lord was amused by the names Adam gave the animals. Can you imagine the chuckle from some of the angels when Adam named the duckbilled platypus? Similarly, in Genesis 2:15, God placed Adam in the garden He had created to "nurture and preserve it." In these examples, we see our Heavenly Father giving Adam a creative role to fulfill with a degree of flexibility. Regarding this ability to create, the early twentieth-century British writer, G.K. Chesterton, in his book *Orthodoxy*, made a point that it is mankind's ability to create that sets us apart from every other creature.

It is instructive that God wanted Adam to name the animals using his own "God given" creativity. Adam likely used this same ingenuity in his caretaking of the garden. I think it is scriptural that our Father, gives us instructions and guidance, but does not necessarily tell us how to do what we are to do. The story of King Saul in First Samuel provides a good illustration of this idea. In verse 10:7, following Samuel's anointing of him the old prophet said, "After you encounter these signs [the locating of his father's donkeys for which he was searching, the meeting of three men who will give him two loaves of bread, and his joining in prophesying with a group of prophets] do what needs to be done based on the situation because God is with you." It seems that Saul was being instructed to use his own understanding to achieve what needed to be done. Nehemiah is another good example of this as he felt prompted to ask the king for a favor to travel to Jerusalem and rebuild the wall. Nehemiah simply prayed for favor, which he received and then did what needed to be done.

The concept of doing what needs to be done rather than taking a prescribed step-by-step procedure is an old principle that many times leads to success. In the early nineteenth century, the German Army developed the concept of "mission tactics," which simply meant that junior officers would accomplish their objectives based on what the situation required. This provided much flexibility in allowing the young officers to be more innovative in achieving the desired results. In the same way, our Heavenly Father has not given us step-by-step procedures; in fact, He prefers we not take such an approach, but rather gives us guidelines and His personal example in our Lord Jesus Christ. Moreover, He has given us all we need to do what needs to be done.

Biblically, our Heavenly Father will never ask us to do anything that He has not first equipped us to do. To illustrate this, there are several scriptures to consider. In Exodus 31, after commanding Moses to build the tabernacle, ark, and different objects, God told Moses that He had given certain men special skills for doing the work He had commanded. God said in verse six, "I am the one who gave special skill to the skillful so they can do all that I expect." In the New Testament, there are several gifts that are spelled out. In Romans twelve, Paul mentions gifts of prophecy, serving others, teaching, the exhortation of others, generosity, leadership, and cheerfully showing mercy to others. Paul continues discussing gifts in First Corinthians twelve, as he spells out the spiritual gifts that are available to us for living lives that are pleasing to God and doing His will. These gifts consist of words of wisdom, words of knowledge, faith, gifts of healing, performing miracles, prophecy, distinguishing spirits, speaking in tongues, and interpretation of tongues. It is important to understand that not everyone has the same gifting, and we should not expect everyone to be the same.

There are many people who are musically talented, and I wish I could be one of them. Music is obviously not my gift, which I learned in high school when I could not keep a beat on the drums. However, I have discovered that the Father gave me other gifts, and He expects me to exercise them. God has given everyone gifts, talents, and abilities, and is watching to see what we do with them. Much like the story of the talents and the three servants who received ten, five and one respectively, our Heavenly Father is eagerly watching to see what we will do with what He has given us. In the parable of the talents, Matthew 25:14-30, I have no doubt the master would have told the servant with the one talent, "Good work, worthy and resolute servant," just as he did to the ones with ten and five, if only that servant had taken the steps to turn the one into two. Moreover, a really industrious servant could have said, "Master, you gave me only one talent, but look, I've made ten more!"

God is pleased when we exercise the skills and abilities He has given us, and scripturally, He is eagerly watching to see what we will do with these gifts. Hebrews 12:1 encourages us, saying, "Since we are surrounded by so many faithful witnesses in heaven, who have gone before us, give up every hindrance and sin that gets in the way and exert more energy in your race,…" This tells me that our Father is keeping an eye on us, along with the saints of old who are cheering us on and watching to see what we will do. Just like I love to see what my grandchildren will do next, and how they will use their ingenuity, the heroes of the faith are all watching us.

Ecclesiastes 9:10 says, "Whatever you are engaged in, do it with all you've got,…" Jesus, in His earthly ministry, was not one to sit idle, and He doesn't want any of us sitting idle either. Life is meant to be lived, and to live is an active verb. Based on the parable of the talents, our Heavenly Father will only be disappointed in us if we do nothing with what He has given us. Even if we fail to achieve our objective, our Father will be pleased. For as God said to David, in Second Chronicles 6:8, regarding his not being able to build the temple, "Because you had it in your heart to do this, you did well." So don't be afraid, go for it; God is watching!

I'm Fixing It!

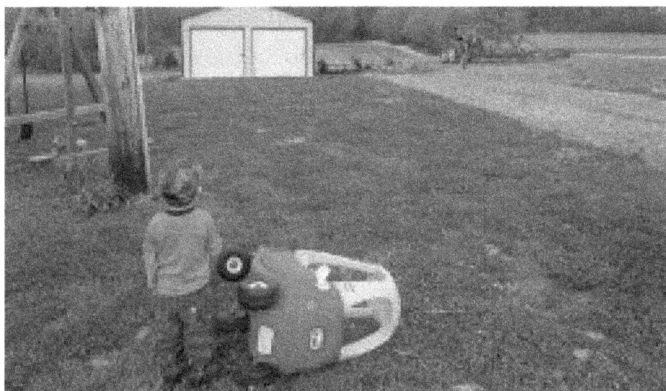

"Stop struggling and recognize that I am God Almighty. I will be highly exalted among all nations and My magnificent glory will cover the earth." Psalm 46:10

"It is futile for you to get up before the sun, and then work late into the night, and wear yourself out; because the Lord gives to the ones He loves even while they are sleeping." Psalm 127:2

Sometimes it seems that JJ was born with a tool in his hand. From his earliest days, JJ has loved tools of all kinds, and he especially loves using them. One day, when he was about three years old, he came walking out of our garage with a screwdriver in his hand. I told him to be careful with it, confident he could not hurt anything. However, within a few minutes, Ella came running to Debi and me saying JJ had broken their little red and yellow car they would play in. Sure enough, JJ had unscrewed the yellow top of the car turning it into a convertible. "I'm fixing it," he said. I could not help but chuckle at this. Then on another memorable day, he again used this phrase.

Whenever Debi is off at an art workshop and I am home alone, I like to visit with the children. Even when I have other things I need to be working on, I'll walk down to JJ and Ella's so I can spend some time with them. On this occasion, JJ was about four, and I noticed him walking toward his gas powered four-wheeler with a wrench in his hand. I didn't think much at the moment but soon realized he had unscrewed the brake line and was draining the fluid. When Mary noticed and took the wrench from him his response was, "I'm fixing it!" I was concerned about the safety factor involved in incidents like this, but again, I had to chuckle. Like JJ and his wrench, how many times have we tried to help our Father by fixing things?

I am confident that our God and Father gave us every tool we need to achieve what He wants us to accomplish. However, it often takes some time and training before we are competent to use His gifts. Moses is an example of trying to "fix it" as JJ would say. When Stephen defended himself before the Council as recorded in Acts 7, he presented an overview of Israel's history. While making his speech, in verse 25, he mentioned that when Moses struck down the Egyptian who had been beating an Israelite, he believed that Israel would recognize him as their deliverer from slavery. As you know, when Moses' deed became known, he had to flee into the wilderness to save his life. Unfortunately, at the time he was not recognized as a liberator. It took 40 years in the wilderness, herding sheep before he was ready for what God wanted him to do. Essentially, Moses was exactly right in his assessment of God's purpose for him but was entirely wrong in his approach. We know from the record in Exodus that while Moses was God's prophet, it was clearly the work of God that delivered Israel.

Our Father loves to make it clear that what is achieved is done by Him and not as a result of our own efforts. The story of King Asa in Second Chronicles 14-16 is an interesting illustration of this. In this narrative, King Asa had an army totaling 580,000 while the opposing force amounted to one million to include 300 chariots. Following Asa's prayer for help, God routed the enemy and brought about a great victory for Judah. However, later when Asa was confronted with the King of Israel, a much smaller force, he paid the King of Syria to attack Israel. There is a stunning lesson here. Asa had prayed for and witnessed a victory over a much larger army but resorted to joining forces with an evil nation to overcome a second, less threatening, opponent. The contrast could not be clearer. In the second instance, Asa was taking steps to "fix it" himself. King Asa was rebuked for this by the prophet who told him that God actively looks for those who trust in Him completely so He can work wonders on their behalf, as the Lord had done previously.

We could also go back to Abraham in the book of Genesis as an example of this. When God did not provide an heir through Sarah as soon as they wanted, Sarah gave her servant Hagar to Abraham to have a son, Ishmael. Again, this is an example of "fixing it." So, how do we know when it is God's time to take action?

The first step, as difficult as it may seem, is to take God at His word. Believing that our Father will do what He promises is not for the weak of heart. The reason for this is that in most cases God acts only when the fulfillment of what was promised is impossible by human reasoning and ability. In the case of Abraham and Sarah, God waited until Abraham was 100 and Sarah was 90 years old! By substituting Hagar for Sarah, they were clearly showing doubt that God was able to fulfill His promise without their help. There are many other examples of how God works on our behalf. In First Kings 18, when the prophet Elijah confronted Israel's false prophets, Elijah drenched the sacrifice in water to the point that it would be impossible to burn it, yet when Elijah prayed The Lord sent down fire to consume everything offered to include the stones. If it doesn't look impossible; generally, God is not interested.

The New Testament presents a more poignant example when Jesus raised Lazarus from the dead. In John 11 Jesus was told that His friend Lazarus was sick, but upon hearing the news, rather than proceeding directly to His sick friend He remained where He was for two additional days. Obviously, Jesus wanted to make sure Lazarus had died even though He told the disciples that Lazarus' sickness would not result in death. For good measure by the time Jesus arrived the body was already in a state of decomposition as Martha was concerned about the odor when Jesus said to remove the stone. In this act, when Lazarus emerged from the tomb, Jesus demonstrated that this was something only God could do. Again, don't look for our Father to do anything that is easy by our standards. Waiting for divine intervention can be nerve racking, but the second step is never to act out of fear.

In First Samuel 13, King Saul was waiting for Samuel to come offer the sacrifice before going into battle with the Philistines. Because Samuel was late in arriving and Israel's army was dwindling, Saul decided to offer the sacrifice himself. As soon as he had completed offering the sacrifice, Samuel arrived and told him that because of this transgression, the kingdom would be given to "a man after God's own heart." Once again King Saul acted out of fear when, in chapter 15, rather than completely destroying Amalek, as God commanded, he kept the best of the spoil and spared the Amalekite King. In this instance when confronted by Samuel, Saul confessed that he was afraid of the people and at their insistence, he did not completely destroy their enemies. King Saul is probably the best example of "fixing it" out of fear that we can find.

When it comes to taking God at His word and refusing to give into fear, I believe Joshua 1:9 says it best; "I have clearly commanded you to be courageous and without fear, because I am going with you wherever you go." We all need to take this to heart and resist the temptation to "fix it" on our own. As our Father has displayed throughout the scriptures, He is capable of far more spectacular results than we can imagine. Also, like JJ fixing his brake line; our actions might not bring about the desired result.

Dandy, Can I Come to Your House?

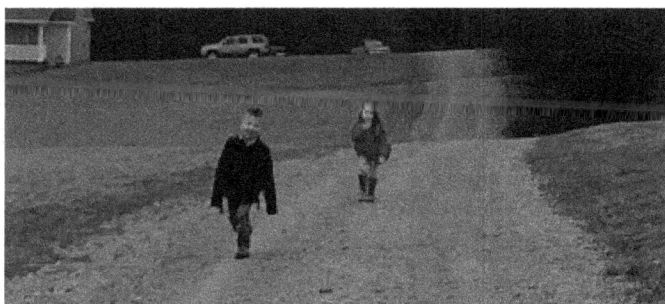

JJ and Ella walking up for a visit.

"Happy is the person You chose to bring close to yourself; to live in your presence." Psalm 65:4

"My inner most being longed to be in the presence of the Lord;" Psalm 84:2

"And I will live in the Lord's palace forever more." Psalm 23:6

"While the young man was still a way off, his father saw him and felt compassion for him, and ran to him and hugged him." Luke 15:20

Because JJ and Ella live very close to Debi and me we frequently get a call in which the first thing we hear after answering is, "Dandy/Granny, can I/we come to your house?" Even when it is not convenient for them to come, I treasure those calls. Sometimes, in the summertime, JJ will sweeten the pot by saying something like, "We need to pull weeds." Of course, as soon as he gets here, I'll say,

"Ready to pull some weeds?" to which he will reply, "Not right now." Life doesn't get much better than these exchanges with our grandchildren because we know they want to be with us. When I get these calls and know they are walking up the gravel road from their house to ours, I go out and watch for them. I enjoy watching them as they get closer and very often, when they see me watching for them they begin running. To think there is anyone in this world who wants to spend time with me like this is extremely moving. Just like JJ and Ella, we can call our Heavenly Father any time and essentially ask if we can come to His House. In fact, just as I watch for my grandchildren, He watches for us to come to Him.

However, our Father does not just watch for us to come to Him; based on Luke 19:10, Jesus came to look for, and find those who were lost. Moreover, Ezekiel 18:23,32 and Second Peter 3:9 make it clear that our Heavenly Father is not pleased with the destruction of even the wicked, and does not want anyone to miss His salvation. Like wisdom personified in Proverbs, God calls out to all who will hear and invites them to His home, and like me watching for JJ and Ella, He watches for all of us.

There are several scriptures that note how God has His eyes on those who seek Him. James 4:8, says that if we "come close to God He will likewise come close to us." Psalm 34:15, says, "The Lord keeps His eyes on those who practice what is pleasing in His sight, and He listens to their concerns." Another passage that has been with me for many years is Second Chronicles 16:9, "The Lord looks all over the earth to find those who are

67

dedicated to Him with all their hearts so He can give them unlimited support." As I watch for JJ and Ella, this passage confirms that God is looking for us to come to Him. There is good reason for every one of us to want to come to our Father.

Some of my favorite Psalms are the ones that describe being in the presence of the Lord. Psalm 16:11 states, "There is complete delight in Your presence, and You have eternal enjoyment in Your right hand." This description should make one wonder why anyone would ever want to leave God's presence! Whenever JJ and Ella come to visit Debi and me there is an anticipation of something good to eat and drink, and that they will be able to engage in activities they love. Many times these expectations include Debi and me playing with them. Very similarly, Psalm 36:8, says, "Those who come to Your house drink as much as they want of Your river of delights." Knowing that there is no limit to our Father's abundance, we should be entering into our Heavenly Father's presence with the same joyful expectation as JJ and Ella coming to our house!

When Jesus encountered the woman at the well in John chapter 4, the woman questioned why He was speaking with her. Jesus responded that He could provide her with "living water." In this exchange, Jesus continued that once drinking this "living water" a person would thirst no more. Similarly, Saint Augustine wrote in his Confessions, "Thou hast created us for Thyself, and our heart is not quiet until it rests in Thee." In other words, we will never be satisfied with anything until we find our satisfaction in Him, and while He prefers that we remain with Him, our Father keeps a watchful eye for those who have wandered away.

I think the parable of the prodigal son is instructive for all of us. As I read the story, it seems the father never stopped watching for his wayward son, longing for the day when he would return. The Old Testament Prophets provide imagery like this as God patiently called Israel and Judah to return to Him. However, there is another story that illustrates the way our Heavenly Father longs for each of us, and that is the story of Absalom, the son of King David.

This story begins in Second Samuel 13 when Absalom murdered his brother Amnon for molesting his sister Tamar. Following the preplanned assassination, Absalom fled to be with his grandfather, Talmai, the King of Geshur. Even though Absalom had murdered his brother, the narrative notes that David's heart longed for Absalom in verse 13:39. After three years, David was convinced to recall his son to Jerusalem, but refused to see him. Next, Absalom was able to engineer his reinstatement back into David's court and began plotting his father's overthrow, which very nearly succeeded. David, his family, and loyal servants had to flee from Jerusalem to escape Absalom and his army. Though Absalom's goal was to kill David, his father, David told his army, as they were about to engage in battle, not to hurt Absalom. However, Joab, the commander of the army, did kill Absalom which resulted in great mourning for King David.

The message of this story is about how strong a father's love can be, even when the child wants to kill him. David refused to give up on Absalom as long as he was alive, and in fact, Second Samuel 18:33 says that as he mourned, David said he would have rather died in Absalom's place. I think we can look at this as foreshadowing our Lord Jesus Christ, who did sacrifice His life for us so that we would not have to die. Just as David never gave up on Absalom as long as he was alive, our Heavenly Father does not give up on us as long as we live. He continues to call out to us through Jesus Christ and the preaching of the Gospel.

Just like Absalom, there is a point of no return for those who continue to reject God's call. That point is when one totally rejects the grace He offers. In this case, such persons, essentially, become strangers to God. My grandchildren are not strangers to me and are welcome in my house any time they like. Similarly, no one should want to be a stranger to God. Thus, the critical question is: Does God know you? For on the day when you do come face to face with Him, you do not want to hear the words, "Go away from me because I have never known you." Hopefully, when you do see Him face to face, He will have His arms wide open as I do for JJ and Ella.

Pick Me Up!

"So I'm telling you, whatever you are praying for believe that you have already received it and it will be given to you." Mark 11:24

"Everything is possible if you believe." Mark 9:23

Taking care of JJ and Ella is always an adventure. Debi and I never know what to expect other than to keep a close eye on them. One day, Debi was away from home while I was entertaining the children. A funny thing about youngsters is the idea that a band-aid will help any booboo. JJ and Ella are no different in this regard. On this particular day, Ella scratched herself and said she needed a band aid. The skin was hardly broken, but to be a good grandfather I went with her to the kitchen and took some band-aids down from a cabinet shelf. Well, wouldn't you know it; these regular bandages were not good enough. She wanted the "Frozen" ones (based on the animated movie Frozen). I just knew we didn't have any band-aids of this type, and accordingly, I told her so. Ella insisted that we did have "Frozen" band-aids, and I insisted again that we did not. Finally, she said, "Pick me up!" "But there aren't any 'Frozen' band-aids there, Ella," I replied. Emphatically, she once again demanded, "Pick me up!" To be honest, she was so cute I could not resist giving in to her demand. So, I picked her up and set her little feet on the counter so she could see for herself. To my surprise, she reached into the back of the cabinet and pulled out some "Frozen" band-aids. My only response was, "What do you know, we do have 'Frozen' band-aids."

Perhaps you would have to be there, but this entire episode was something I thanked God for. Moreover, for a long time, I struggled with the lesson to be learned here. Though I knew that God was using Ella to get my attention, I just wasn't sure what it was. As I studied the scriptures and prayed about the lesson, it hit me; it is all about faith! In Mark 9:23, Jesus told the demon-possessed boy's wavering father, "Everything is possible if you believe." For Ella, she had no doubt there were "Frozen" band-aides in the cabinet, and though I tried to dissuade her, she persisted in her confident belief they were there. How many times have each of us been like the father of the demon-possessed child in the Gospel of Mark and prayed, "If You can?" I am convinced that our Heavenly Father wants us to be as confident as Ella when we come to Him.

I realize there are many people out there praying to win the lottery or the Publisher's Clearing House Sweepstakes. In these situations, I'm not so sure God wants us to exhibit this kind of confidence, even though in our own minds we know we can use the winnings for good causes. Our Lord Jesus told the disciples in John 16:24, "In the past, you have not asked for anything in My name, but I'm telling you now to ask and I'll give it to you so that you can have complete joy." So how does this passage square with the reality of asking and receiving? I think it begins with the realization of what kind of people we are called to be.

In Luke 9:54, after a Samaritan village rejected Jesus, His disciples, James and John, suggested they should call down fire from heaven to consume the inhospitable village. Depending on the translation you may be using, in verses 55-56, Jesus rebuked them, and said they did not know what spirit they were of and that He did not come to destroy but to save. Clearly, in this case, the disciples were not aware of how they were called to respond. In their minds, they were supposed to be like the Old Testament Prophet Elijah, who did call fire down from heaven to consume his enemies. Based on this example, it is important to understand our callings and what we should have faith in. Much like the well-known passage in Proverbs 3:5-6, Psalm 37:4-5 says,

"Take pleasure in the Lord and He will grant the longings of your innermost being. Promise to follow in the Lord's steps, and have confidence in Him, and He will make it come to pass." The thing I get from this is that if we are earnestly seeking our Heavenly Father, he will place desires in our hearts, and that as we follow Him, he will make these wishes happen. In the context of these and other scriptures, it is hard for me to see God giving someone a winning lottery ticket just because they are reading their Bible. However, I will admit that it could happen. The thing I do interpret from these passages is that when we have a close relationship with God, the things near to His heart will be near to ours, and these are the things we will be seeking.

Proverbs 13:20 says, "Anyone who spends time with wise people will themselves become wise." The truth of this proverb should be self-evident. It is also a well-known saying that "You are known by the company you keep." The people we spend the most time with and the thoughts that we feed upon contribute to the making of our character. Thus, it should be no surprise that as we spend time with our Heavenly Father by reading and learning the Bible and in prayer, we will become more like Him and, in fact, be taking pleasure in Him.

As Paul pointed out in First Corinthians 2:12, we have received the Holy Spirit from God so that we can know all the things He has freely given us. Think about this. We can have the same thoughts as God. Some people will consider this far-fetched and wishful thinking, but this is what the Bible says. Jesus, Himself told the disciples that He would ask the Father to send the Holy Spirit to us to remind us of everything He said. In my life, it has not been uncommon for a verse of scripture or a scripturally based image to come to mind when I needed encouragement or direction.

Many years ago as a young lieutenant in the Air Force I was placed in a position I had a hard time adjusting to. Following a particularly difficult week, I knew my job security was at risk. In fact, I was pretty sure I would be fired from this particular job. In the military, getting fired from a job does not mean you will be unemployed, but that you will be moved down to a lesser job. This is what you would refer to as a career killer. It was on a Saturday that I reflected on events, and thought to myself, "I'm dead." Immediately following this, in my mind, I saw a ripe wheat field with a gentle breeze blowing over the heads of grain, and the question came to mind, "What does God do with the dead?" That was very encouraging, though the following Monday, I did get the bad news that I was to be fired. However, almost immediately things began to change, to the point that Friday afternoon, I was asked to remain in my position. You might say I was raised from the dead. Much like Ella, my Heavenly Father picked me up.

Our Father is looking for those who will be bold enough to ask Him to pick them up. Before anyone can be this bold, he or she must first have a relationship with Him in which that person has the confidence to make that request. Ella has spent enough time with Debi and me that she can, at any time, say, "Pick me up!" As we examine ourselves, it is a good thing to ask, how much time have we spent with our Father?

I Love You Too, Dandy

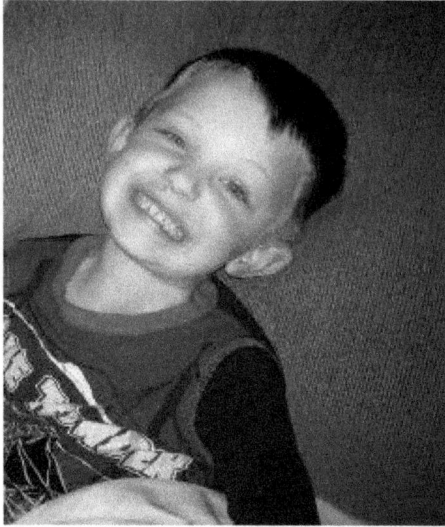

"I love you, Lord, you are the source of my strength." Psalm 18:1

"Never stop loving the Lord, all of you who walk in His ways!" Psalm 31:23

"O how I love the Lord because He listens for my voice and for my requests." Psalm 116:1

Even though JJ lived with us for the first two years of his life he has always enjoyed spending the night with Debi and me. Oftentimes, he and Ella will both stay with us. These are special times when we will usually watch a movie of their choosing, and Debi will make some popcorn. Usually, they want to do anything Debi and I do, so before bedtime, they like to brush their teeth with us (they keep bushes at our house). After brushing teeth, Ella will want to sleep with Debi, while JJ will want to sleep with me. They are both restless sleepers, and I can't tell you the number of times I have awakened with two little feet pushing me out of the bed. I remember one night in particular when JJ was about four years old that as we turned out the lights, I said, "I love you, JJ," to which he replied, "I love you too, Dandy." I believe everyone has had the experience in which someone says something in just the right way that touches the heart. This was one of those times for me. This was also one of those times in which I could sense the Lord saying, "It's okay for you to tell Me that you love Me too."

I'm afraid that many of us go through life and never take time to tell those who are closest to us how much they mean to us and that we love them. As I've grown older, it has become more and more important to me to tell those who have been especially meaningful to me that I love them. Love is, at best, a nebulous word filled with uncertain meanings. I love Debi, and I love my best friends from different times in my life. I love all of my children and grandchildren, and I also love pizza and my car. These are clearly different kinds of love that require some distinction. C.S. Lewis masterfully covered these in his book, *The Four Loves*, which I highly recommend if you have not read it. My treatment of the topic will be much briefer. Suffice it to say that I understand the differences and that loving my grandchildren is an entirely new area.

The fact is, there is nothing I would not do for them that is within my ability to accomplish. I am constantly concerned with their health, safety, and well-being, and I love to be near them. If I had to do it I would sacrifice my life for them as I would have for their parents. That is how much I love them.

All my desires and concerns for my grandchildren imperfectly describe our Heavenly Father's love for each of us. He was not just willing to die for us; He gave His Son Jesus Christ to die in our place so we could be near Him. Essentially, our Father went far beyond words to demonstrate His perfect and complete love for us. As Deuteronomy 6:5 says, it should be a natural response on our part to "love our God with all our heart, with our entire mind and with our every ounce of strength." As I want to be close to my grandchildren, I hope that they will want to be close to me. In God's case, what more can He do?

At this point in my life, I tend to look at the world as a message from God. Since that night with JJ, I frequently notice something, a bird chirping, a cool summer breeze, or the fragrance of spring flowers, and my response is, "I love you too, Father." I believe God wants to hear us tell Him how much we love Him, but the real statement has to be in actions. John 14:21 says, "The person who observes and performs my commandments is the one who loves Me, and whoever loves Me, My Father will love, and I will love that person and make myself known to him or her." When Jesus speaks of His commandments in this passage, it is important to realize that it all comes down to one very simple commandment: love one another (John 13:34-35).

Our love for God is evident only to the degree we love others. In First John 4:20, he put it this way, "you cannot hate the brother or sister you have seen with your eyes, and love the God you have never seen with your eyes." Love for your neighbor is a consistent theme throughout the scriptures. Jesus taught in Matthew 22:37-39 that the greatest commandment was to love God with your whole being and your neighbor as yourself. This is also spelled out in detail in the Old Testament law. For example, Numbers 23:4 says, "If you notice that the ox or donkey belonging to someone you don't like is wandering away, you are responsible for returning the ox or donkey to that person." There are many passages similar to this scattered throughout the scriptures in which God instructs us to essentially treat others the way we want to be treated. Thus, the degree of our love for our Heavenly Father is evident to the degree that we demonstrate our love for others.

While I take every opportunity to make my grandchildren happy and secure, much of this is conveyed through words. Very often, I hug JJ and say, "Do you know I love you?" Just as often, he replies, "Always." I have to admit that this is a response that touches me every time, and I believe we should be responding in this way to our Heavenly Father. Still, this brings up the question: are we always convinced of God's love? Jesus' sacrifice for us should, in itself, be enough for us to exclaim that we always, without a doubt, know He loves us. However, as I have learned, life in this world does not always lend itself as a reminder of God's great love. Every one of us goes through trials and uncertain times, which will make us doubt if we allow them to. My trials have ranged from difficulties at my work to the loss of a child. In each and every case, I never doubted that God was aware of the circumstance and in control. While there was a degree of suffering, knowing God's involvement made it more bearable. I believe it was with this in mind that in John 16:33, Jesus said, "I've told you all this so that you will have peace in Me. You are going to have hard times in this world, but be bold and daring in your faith because I have overcome the world." Knowing always that He loves us should be enough for each of us to live confidently, and in a way that demonstrates our love for others, which is essentially saying, "I love you too Father."

We Know Who's Driving the Zero Turn

"While people think they are deciding on how to proceed, it is really the Lord who directs them." Proverbs 16:9

"It is the Lord who decides which way someone will go, so how can anyone possibly understand their path?" Proverbs 20:24

"You O Lord will direct my steps with Your perfect guidance, and in the end, You will bring me home; into Your glory." Psalm 73:24

Because we live far out in the country in a rural community, we have a large yard that demands a significant amount of time during the growing season. The yard is more than two acres, and being a little on the obsessive-compulsive side, I can't stand for it to look poorly kept. A tool that makes the job much easier and more enjoyable is a zero-turn mower. Of course, JJ wants to help as often as he can. When he was just over a year old I would take him out and let him steer our tractor in the field. JJ is a natural when it comes to anything with an engine and wheels. It must run in the family, as the same is true for his uncle CJ and cousin, Brandon. Just as JJ loves his motorized vehicles, he is also interested in our zero-turn mower. Whenever he sees me in the yard mowing, he always wants to ride with me. On these occasions, when he is with me, I lengthen the seatbelt to hold us both in, and I also let him hold the bars that steer the mower. Though on these occasions, JJ is holding the means of control, I've always been the one who actually steers.

One day after mowing the yard, I commented to Debi that JJ had fun and thought he was driving the zero-turn. As we talked about our little man, it occurred to me that so often we really think we are in control of our lives when someone else is actually steering our course. As a result of this, when discussing the future, Debi and I frequently add that we know who's really driving the zero-turn. We all spend our lives believing that we are in control and, as some like to quip, "we make our own luck." As someone who studies future techniques and ways of analyzing future possibilities, I often advise people on decision-making and planning. While I emphasize our responsibility in forming the future we will inherit, there still remains the invisible hand of God that opens and closes doors and directs us in the path we take. We can do this consciously or unconsciously.

As an example of consciously accepting God's guidance, consider Proverbs 3:5-6. "With all your heart, trust in the Lord, and do not depend on your own ideas of how things should be. With every step, admit that God is in charge, and He will tell you which way to go." The best Biblical example of this is Abraham. All his life, he followed God's instructions to the point of demonstrating a willingness to sacrifice his only, promised son. The result of Abraham's obedience and willingness to follow God closely is that he developed a unique and close relationship with God Almighty. Moreover, in terms of worldly wealth, he was one of the richest men to ever live. Abraham is an example of someone consciously choosing to follow God. Many times, we fail to deliberately follow God, so the result is that He directs things differently than we would expect.

The Old Testament character Joseph provides an excellent illustration of how God directs our steps when we are largely unaware of what is going on. When reading Genesis 37, it appears Joseph was set up from the beginning. First, his father Jacob showed favoritism by giving him a special multicolored coat. As you would imagine, this did not endear him to his brothers. Then, Joseph had a couple of fantastic dreams about his personal exaltation, which caused even more resentment on the part of his brothers. The result of all this was that Joseph's brothers sold him into slavery, and he was taken to Egypt. To explain their missing brother, Joseph's siblings led their father Jacob to believe he had been killed by a wild animal. In Egypt, Joseph, true to his faith in God, maintained his integrity and resisted the sexual advances of his master's wife. When she falsely accused him, he ended up in prison for over two years! Finally, Joseph was recognized for his administrative ability and made the ruler over Egypt. Now how does that happen?

Think about the possible path for Joseph's life. Had he remained with his family he would have become a successful shepherd at best. But because God was "steering the zero-turn," Joseph went through years of trial and not only became ruler of Egypt, but he also saved his family and a lot of other lives. If we could go back and ask Joseph if he wished things had been different, what do you think he would have said? Regardless of the suffering he went through, I believe Joseph was pretty satisfied in the end. I believe it was with this in mind that Paul said in Romans 8:28, "It is well known that God makes everything work for the good of those who love Him, and He calls into His service."

Another example I would point out is King David. Think about his life for a moment based on the narrative in First Samuel 16-31. As a young boy, he was anointed King of Israel. Then he went out and slew a giant that everyone else was afraid to face. Follow this up with leading the army to more victories, and it would seem he was in the driver's seat. However, because of King Saul's jealousy, David spent years on the run as a fugitive. Then, following the burning of his town, Ziklag, his own men wanted to stone him. I bet David was thinking, "It wasn't supposed to be this way!" Still, very soon after recovering all that was lost in Ziklag, he did become king. So many times, we go through a rough patch and wonder why we are going through it. Yet there is a common element in Joseph, and David, as well as many other heroes of the Bible.

The common element is an unwavering commitment to God. In Joseph's case, this was the reason he went to prison. As recounted in the narrative in Genesis 39:9, when the wife of Potiphar, his master, made sexual advances toward him, he responded saying, "I cannot commit an evil of this nature and sin against God." In First Samuel 24:4-6 and 26:6-12 David maintained the same commitment as a fugitive when he twice refused to kill King Saul, but rather trusted God to take care of the matter. Both these stories seem to be examples of Proverbs 3:5-6. "With all your heart, trust in the Lord, and do not depend on your own ideas of how things should be. With every step, admit that God is in charge, and He will tell you which way to go."

For me, it has been a comfort to know who is in charge and is directing events in my life as well as in the world. In my career as a military officer and as a teacher, I can say that the situations that were most uncomfortable for me effectively prepared me for higher positions and greater responsibilities. As Proverbs 20:24 says, "It is the Lord who decides which way someone will go, so how can anyone possibly understand their path?" You may not understand the way things are headed, but you can confidently know who is driving the zero-turn.

Hitting the Target

"God clearly showed His great love for us, because while we were still lost sinners Christ died for each of us." Romans 5:8

"God made Jesus, who never sinned, to be sin for our benefit so that we can be blameless children of God through what Jesus did." Second Corinthians 5:21

It seemed like JJ wanted to be with his dad and me from the very beginning. If one of us did something, JJ thought he was supposed to be doing it. We are a sporting family and enjoy marksmanship. JJ was four years old and, of course, he wanted to shoot at targets just like Jerry and me. I decided one Saturday to take JJ to a turkey shoot. I think most people know exactly how a turkey shoot works, but for anyone who is unfamiliar with these contests, participants shoot at targets, and the best shot wins the frozen turkey. In preparation for this event, I bought JJ a small 410-gauge shotgun. When I went to pick him up, JJ was as excited as a young boy could be. He was with his Dandy and some of Dandy's friends. When we arrived at the turkey shoot, I realized that JJ's short barrel was not sufficient to get the game shot to the target. I did not want JJ to be disappointed, so I began shooting at his target. I confess that other participants gave me some strange looks when there was not a mark on my target, but JJ was filled with satisfaction at all the holes in his. The end result was that JJ went home with a turkey!

The great lesson here, and one that means so much to me, is that our Heavenly Father, through Jesus Christ, hits the target that we cannot possibly reach. In First Peter 1:16, the author quoted Leviticus 11:44, "I want you to be holy because I am holy." I've been a student of the Bible for many years and only recently began wondering exactly what it means to be holy. Of course, I've always known that holiness expresses trying to live according to Biblical principles, as well as religious sacredness, and thoughts of God, but my belief is that it goes far beyond our comprehension. I recently asked a Bible scholar friend of mine what he thought holy meant, and his description was, "Wow!" So, what makes up wow? Based on what God told Moses in Exodus, because He is holy, He is unapproachable. For example, in Exodus 33:20, God tells Moses, "No one can set eyes on Me and live." Now, this conveys "wow!" To actually see true holiness is fatal to humans. In my own mind, I describe holiness as without flaw, perfectly consistent in purpose, complete, and lacking nothing. This definition, if it can be so called, makes it obvious to me that I have missed the mark.

Our creator and Heavenly Father set such a high bar for us that meeting this expectation is unattainable. There are so many areas in which I have been less than holy that I wouldn't know where to start in trying to get to that place. Another problem that I see is that in being perfectly consistent in purpose, God does not let the guilty go unpunished, as He told Moses in Exodus 34:7. We all love those passages that describe God's love, compassion, mercy, and provision, but punishment is another matter. Yet the good news is that God, through our Lord Jesus Christ, hit the mark we could never hope to come near! Jesus gave us the prize that He won!

God wants us to be with Him so much, He was willing to sacrifice His only, without flaw, perfectly consistent in purpose, complete and lacking nothing, Son. This is truly remarkable. It seems to me that it would have been so much easier to entirely wipe out the human race and start over with some creatures that could attain the goal. Rather than discarding all of us, God's solution was to redeem us.

As I think back on my time at the turkey shoot with JJ, I realize that I would rather give up some time with my friends and winning a turkey just to have my little man with me. If I can be said to have a sincere love for my grandson, how much greater is God's love for each of us. Our Father wants us to be with Him and enjoy being with Him. He also wants each of us to have a sense of achievement and satisfaction. As I learned while watching JJ and Ella play, God has given us the talents and skills for various activities. Moreover, He has given us the opportunity to engage in these activities. The writer of Ecclesiastes, in verse 5:19, put it this way, "For every person who has received abundance and affluence from God, He has additionally enabled those people to enjoy, and have that abundance as a return for their labors. This is indeed a present from the hand of God."

In the case of JJ and the turkey shoot, there was no way he would be able to adequately hit the target, much less win a turkey. This is the case with us; there is just no way that we can, on our own, make ourselves acceptable to God. If we could make our own way, then Jesus died for no good reason. The fact still remains that we all missed the mark and missed it early in our lives. In Matthew chapter five, Jesus lays out some pretty stringent statements. For example, calling someone a "fool" is essentially equated with murder, and looking lustfully at someone is the same as adultery. Thus, we are held liable for more than our misdeeds; we are accountable for every thought! Who can survive under these kinds of expectations? The good news is that, as the Apostle Paul said in Romans 5:15, "But the free gift is unlike the transgression. Because if many people died because of the transgression of one person [Adam], then the wonderful gift of God's grace through our Lord Jesus Christ overflows to so many more."

Again, as I reflect on this, I can't help but think back to that turkey shoot. It comes down to this.

Our Father takes us to the event to be with Him. He provides all that we need to participate. But even more wonderful, He wins the prize for us.

The Gifts

"When Jesus saw a poor widow give two half pennies, He told his disciples, "This poor widow gave more to the temple offering than all the others, because they all gave out of their plenty, but she has given out of her lack, putting in everything she had."" Mark 12:42-44

"The Lord loves a happy giver." 1 Corinthians 9:7

"The Lord has made it perfectly clear what is acceptable. All He wants from you is to be fair and impartial to all, to treasure kindheartedness for others, and be in constant communion with Him." Micah 6:8

I had just celebrated my birthday, which came and went with no fanfare. At my age, it is enough to say I made it. Then Mary brought JJ and Ella over to stay with Debi and me for the evening. JJ walked in saying, "Here you go Dandy. This is for your birthday." I looked to see a plastic Ziploc bag containing a padlock with keys, a few dollar bills, and some change. I told JJ, "Thank you," then asked Mary if she had put him up to this. Mary assured me that she merely mentioned that it was my birthday, and he did this on his own. This gift was more meaningful to me than any great gift anyone could ever give me, and the reason has to do with the things JJ treasures.

There are several things that have special meaning to my grandson, and two of them are padlocks and money. Strange as it may sound to some people, JJ loves padlocks and keys. He has an impressive collection for a boy of his age. Next, like his cousin Brandon, he collects money. I confess we do pay him when he gets good grades, and he is quick to remind us when we forget. He even has his own cash box in which he keeps his collection of currency. Since I no longer anticipate birthday gifts, and actually I do not encourage them, JJ especially touched me by giving me things that he holds dear. This was an occasion in which it truly was the thought that counted most, and this gift will always be special to me.

The natural question for me is: if JJ's gift to me was so moving, what meaningful thing can we give our Heavenly Father, someone who quite literally has everything? Well, the obvious answer is that God wants us, our hearts, souls, minds, and strength. I think the first answer to this has to do with what is meaningful to me. Biblically fasting, doing without food or something else, is a form of worship and seeking God. In this case, food is certainly meaningful to all of us, and doing without it can be a significant sacrifice, but not necessarily.

In answer to the question of what to bring before the Lord, the prophet Micah, in verse 6:8, says, "The Lord has made it perfectly clear what is acceptable. All He wants from you is to be fair and impartial to all, to treasure kindheartedness for others, and be in constant communion with Him." This one passage makes it pretty simple what is most dear to God's heart. Based on what Jerimiah 9:24 says, we know that God exercises lovingkindness, justice, and righteousness. These are essentially the same things Micah says God wants from us.

The only conclusion that I can draw from the scriptures is that God wants us to be in His image. We find the same thought in Deuteronomy 10:12, which says, "What does the Lord God expect from you, Israel, except to be in continuous reverent awe of Him, and to strive to be like Him, and love Him, and serve Him with your whole being, and to do what He has told you this day for your benefit." Both of my sons live in States different from where Debi and I live, so we are not able to see them as often as we would like. We were visiting one of them on Father's Day weekend a few years ago, and went to Sunday morning services with him. When he introduced us to his pastor, the pastor exclaimed, "I wish I had fifty more like your son." When Debi and I returned home, I visited my own father, who lives nearby, and told him that it was the greatest Father's Day gift I could have received. When we are going about as our Heavenly Father's representatives on earth, and engaging with Him in every endeavor, we are giving Him the greatest gift we have to give.

There is an old saying that, "You can't out-give the giver." Essentially, this means we can't give God more than He has given us. But what we can do is express gratitude for the multitude of gifts He has lavished upon us. In this regard, another time a gift made an impression on me was the Christmas following my birthday. As Debi and I prepared for gift buying, JJ told us he wanted a toolbox. This seemed like an easy enough request, so Debi and I went to a tool store and found him a red metal toolbox. In addition to this, we bought him several other gifts to include an actual tool set. I was surprised on Christmas day when he opened his gifts, for he was most impressed with the red toolbox. As he carefully put tools from the toolset into the box, he said, "This is special." I can tell you that my heart warmed when I heard him say this. Furthermore, I know that our Heavenly Father loves to hear us tell Him that His many gifts to us are special.

My son-in-law, Jerry, has quite a knack for building and repairing things. He is frequently working on his truck or making something for Mary in his spare time. Similar to Jerry, I too have some inclination for woodworking and designing furniture and buildings. As you can see, JJ, from the very beginning, caught on that working with tools is something that he should be doing. In fact, we have to keep a close eye on him because with a screwdriver in hand, he would disassemble every toy! Thus, the thought that the toolbox was a special gift for JJ adds a little more meaning to what I believe God was teaching me. The reason the toolbox is special is that it and the tools in it provide him with the means for being like his dad and me. So what has our Heavenly Father given us that is comparable to JJ's toolbox?

There are two things that are most precious to me, which are the Holy Spirit and the Bible. Jesus said in John 14:18, "I am not going to leave you alone like children with no parents." Here, He was speaking of the Holy Spirit that He would send after He had ascended to Heaven. Jesus went on to say in verse 26 that the Holy Spirit would teach us and remind us of everything He said. Thus, this is how God communicates with us-through the Holy Spirit. The next most precious thing to me is the Bible. As a young man, I began memorizing scriptures. At the time, it was a good mental exercise for building a disciplined mind. Moreover, in counseling others, I usually had a scripture, appropriate to their situation, to share. However, as I grew older, I realized that these scriptures I had memorized became a method of communication for the Holy Spirit to speak to me.

A passage of particular importance has been Joshua 1:9, that says, "You know that I have told you to be mighty, and courageous because I the Lord your God am with you wherever you go." When Debi and I married, our pastor, Dr. William L. Lane, reinforced this in the message he shared with us by saying, "God is with you." I am happy to report this has been the case for over 40 years. There are many other scriptures that come to mind to encourage and direct me. The wonderful thing is this is my Heavenly Father's way of speaking to me. This precious gift from God enables everyone who has a relationship with Him to be our gift to Him. This gift is to become like our Lord in this world. Like JJ, I can truly say, "This is special."

Time Out!

"Happy is the one You Lord correct, and who you instruct from your principles." Psalm 94:12

"Our Lord disciplines everyone He loves, and those He accepts as His children, He strongly corrects." Hebrews 12:6

Well, this is a chapter I just wasn't sure I wanted to tackle; grandparents correcting their grandchildren? Such things should not be! Still, the more I thought about it and considered its importance, I could not escape the belief that it needed to be done. Anytime JJ and Ella come to visit, they do so with the expectation of fun. This is one of the aspects of grand parenting that makes it so worthwhile. I'm sure you have heard the adages about spoil them then send them home. That is how it should be. Nevertheless, because Debi and I do live nearby and spend considerable time with JJ and Ella, we have to take a role in teaching them. This includes the discipline part of it.

Sometimes getting JJ to listen and obey is harder than others. On one particular spring day, we were outside, and he and Ella were playing on a rope swing. As I was pushing Ella on the swing, JJ grabbed a low-hanging limb and began tearing leaves off of it. Since leaves on a tree look good and provide shade on hot days, I told him to stop ripping the leaves off. At the time, he was not open to obeying Dandy, so I repeated the instruction several times. When he continued to refuse to comply with my request, I had to take action that involved discipline. To avoid doing anything, I tried to rationalize that it really didn't matter. Then it occurred to me that it mattered that he be responsive to my voice.

Many years ago, when our children were small, we lived in Colorado, and we would often go hiking in the mountains. One weekend, we were on a trail that went across a road, and our son Michael, four years old at the time, raced out ahead of us downhill toward the road. While there was not a lot of traffic on this road, there were cars on it. As Michael neared the road, I noticed a car moving on an intercept course with our son. I immediately yelled, "Michael, stop!" Sure enough, he stopped, and slid to the edge of the road, barely missing the oncoming car. This is an example of why our children and grandchildren need to be responsive to our voice. Several years later, Michael provided another example of the need to obey.

When Michael was about seven or eight years old he loved to whittle with knives-much like JJ now. I had a Swiss army knife that I gave him and told him to be very careful. "Always cut away from yourself and never dig into the wood with your knife because the blade will fold on you and cut you." This was on a Sunday. The very next day, as I was returning home from work, driving through our neighborhood, I passed Debi and the children. Our oldest son, CJ stuck his head out of the van window and said, "We're taking Mike to the hospital because he cut himself." Sure enough, he had done what I instructed him not to do. He started digging with the knife and the blade folded on him. Fortunately, it was not bad though it did require a couple of stitches. When I saw Michael he looked up and asked, "Dad, are you going to spank me?" "No son," I replied, "I'm not going to spank you. I just wish you had obeyed me and not cut yourself." This is all our Heavenly Father wants. He wants to spare us from unnecessary pain.

Whether it is JJ and Ella or their mom and uncles before them, the purpose of all instruction and discipline is to prevent harm from coming to them. There have been times when JJ or Ella have become too rambunctious and hurt themselves. Each time, seeing them in any kind of pain, makes me wish I could reach out and take it from them. This is what our Heavenly Father has done for us. Through Jesus Christ, He has suffered so we will not have to. When we have entered into this kind of relationship with our Heavenly Father, He takes special interest in us

100

to keep us on the right path. I have had this experience in my own life.

As a young man, there was a time I had become haughty and thought a little more of myself than I should have. I had finished my master's degree and begun my Air Force career. For the first three years, I felt like I could not fail, and considered few others up to my level of ability. Even worse, while I was very active in the chapel program and actually taught Bible classes, I felt like I had personally arrived. As educated as I was, it seems I had forgotten Proverbs 6:16-19, which lists "a haughty look" as one of the six things the Lord hates. At the time, I had a good job when a position at the headquarters opened up. "That's where I need to be," I thought, "working with the generals." I got the job, and it was the most humbling experience of my life! For the first time in my short career, I could do nothing right. In the first week, I learned that sharp as I might have thought I was, I was not prepared for this position. What a mistake! Even worse, as noted in a previous chapter, I was fired then rehired, and I continued to pay for this mistake for the next 18 months. I learned humility!

Like my extensive lesson in humility, our Heavenly Father will do what needs to be done to help each of us conform to His kingdom. The wonderful thing is that He did not let me go saying something like, "He's clearly not worth it." God took the time to teach me what I was missing in my development as one of His children. Verse four of the twenty-third Psalm, says "your rod and staff comfort me." The rod and staff are tools of correction to keep the sheep where they are supposed to be. To illustrate, there is an old book, entitled *The Shepherd Psalm: A Meditation*, that was written by William Evans in 1921. In this book, he recounted the story of a shepherd who intentionally broke the leg of one of his sheep. The reason for this, the shepherd explained, was that this was a sheep that tended to wander off on its own and, in fact, would lead other sheep off as well. Moreover, this particular sheep would not come close to the shepherd. To remedy this problem, the shepherd broke its leg and then carefully reset it. Of course, this resulted in the sheep having to lie down for several days, and it had to take its food from the shepherd's hand. This cured the sheep from wandering off and made it closer to the shepherd.

Any time our Heavenly Father corrects us, no matter how painful it may seem at the time, the desired result is that we come closer to Him and become more responsive to His voice. Whenever I have to correct JJ or Ella, my heart's desire is for them to come closer to me. This is a closeness that is not based on fear, but an acknowledgment that I love them and will take every necessary step possible to keep them safe and happy. As Jesus said in John 10:27, "Those who are of My flock are familiar with My voice, and I know each of them by name, and they closely follow Me." This is a passage that should comfort each one of us, just realizing that He knows us. With the billions of people in this world, not to mention managing the entire universe, your Heavenly Father still knows you personally and wants to spend one-on-one time with you. What an awesome God!

Boo Boos

The nail I shot myself with.

"He was cut through for our wrongdoings, He was overwhelmed because of our crimes, He suffered judgment to give us comfort and security, and because of the torments He endured, we can be made well." Isaiah 53:5

In my home study, I have a loft that serves as a reading nook and something of a place for prayer; a "war room," if you will. On the wall of the loft, there is a small walnut plaque holding a rusty nail. There is a story behind the nail, the short of which is that when I was framing the loft, I accidentally nailed two of my fingers together with a nail gun. I saved the nail after the doctor removed it and attached it to this block as a reminder of what can happen if you're not careful. Shooting myself with the nailer was not the most painful event of my life. It merely makes for an unusual story. The most painful events have to do with my children and grandchildren.

While we lived in Japan, Debi gave birth to our third son, Lionel. Just like CJ and Michael,

Lionel was a source of great joy for Debi and me. We really went overboard, buying infant clothing with lion patterns, lion toys, and filling his room with stuffed lions. We looked forward to seeing him grow up with his big brothers. However, Lionel developed an ear infection that turned into meningitis, which took his life when he was only four months old. This was by far the most traumatic pain we had endured.

There were other incidents to tear at our hearts. I remember CJ's first bicycle accident, in which he knocked out a tooth. Then there was the time Mary fell out of a tree and knocked out five teeth. You've already read about Michael and the knife. Child rearing is not for the faint of heart. Moreover, painful moments do not go away when the children leave home, and in some ways, it hurts more when it happens to grandchildren. Our oldest grandson, Brandon, for example, has had more than his share of injuries on and off the sports field, that because of the distance Debi and I only heard about. Then there is JJ and Ella.

When our little Ella was about two years old, she developed meningitis, the same type that took Lionel from us. Mary and Jerry were still living in our apartment at the time, so Debi and I were extremely close and very concerned. As so often happens with these cases, it takes the doctors a while to figure out what is going on. To this day, fearful with a shudder, I give thanks to God that they realized what she had soon enough to not only save her life but to prevent permanent damage. The experience was much too close for comfort.

One day JJ and Ella were running around on our hardwood floors in their stocking feet. As JJ careened through the living room, his feet slid to the side, and he hit his head on the corner of a table. Debi and I were able to comfort him, and he was back at it soon enough. Later that day, I spoke with my brother-in-law, Lester, and described the incident. Without much thought, I added, "I would rather drive a nail through my hand than see my children hurt." It soon occurred to me that I described how our Heavenly Father feels about us.

One of the oldest discussions in the world has to do with why evil exists, and if God is so good, why He doesn't stop it. If millennia of theologians and philosophers can't adequately address this, there is no way I can do it justice in this short space. However, over the years, I have learned a few things that comfort me regarding this issue. The first thing has to do with choice.

In Genesis chapter two, God gave Adam and Eve a choice to obey or not to obey a simple restriction. Based on deceptive persuasion from the serpent, they chose to disobey. In this act, they unleashed all evil as we know it today to include meningitis that has struck and threatened our family. Throughout the scriptures, people were given choices. For example, Joshua 24:15 says, "Choose today who you will serve." There are other examples of good choices and bad. The tremendous latitude God has given the human race enables each of us to make the best of decisions and the worst. Unfortunately, these decisions have ripple effects far beyond ourselves. For example, a child growing up in a dysfunctional and unloving home may give in to a life of crime, the seeds of which were sown by the parents. In the case of nations, those who support the rise of dictators for whatever reason can contribute to the suffering and death of millions, as was the case leading up to World War Two. So, my understanding is that the problem of evil began with the first lie and bad choice and has been exponentially multiplied though more individual and group choices. Essentially, the problem has to do with free will. So what has our loving Heavenly Father done to alleviate this suffering?

The answer is simple: God chose to suffer with us. Unsophisticated as this statement may seem, it is packed with meaning. First, consider that God, who is all-powerful, all-knowing, and everywhere present, could have handled this problem any way He wanted. I suppose it is not too much to believe that God could have, in some way, just made evil go away. That would be easy enough for someone who is all-powerful. However, our Father through Jesus Christ chose to suffer with us. Why? For me, the best answer is that we would never know the incredible depth of His love in any other way. In those instances in which JJ or Ella hurt themselves, all I can do is hold them close and sometimes tell them of a time when something similar happened to me. Heck, I shot myself with a nail gun! Essentially, we are dealing with compassion.

The word compassion essentially means to suffer with someone. In our case, the best we can do is to be with and try to comfort one another during difficult times. However, in the case of our Heavenly

Father, through Jesus Christ, He did come down and suffer with us as prophesied in Isaiah 53:5. Because of this, we know that He loves us enough to suffer as a human being. Yet the aspect of our Lord's suffering was not an end in itself; it was for the payment and forgiveness of our sins. The end result was that we can look forward to the rest of eternity, which is a very long time, with Him. Our God loves us that much. I would gladly suffer myself to relieve my grandchildren's pain, but I can't do it. Our God did do it. The relief, however, is not physical; it is in the knowledge that He cares, and we are following in His steps. Jesus told the disciples in John 16:33 that He knew we would have troubles in this life. Still, He did not stop at that, for He wants us to be encouraged by the fact that He overcame the world and its evils.

Boo boos are small aspects of the evils we must endure in this world. Some of them will be small, and some can be major. So often, the best thing we can do is to be there for our children, grandchildren, and each other. This is exactly what our God has done for us. He came close enough to suffer with us.

Stay with Me, Dandy

"I might even walk through a deep dark valley surrounded by the threat of death, but as long as You are with me I have nothing to fear." Psalm 23:4

As is the case with all young children, when entering a dark room or thinking about being alone, they often want an adult to stay with them. I have noticed that JJ and Ella want either Debi or me to be with them when they are entering a dark room, and often want us to remain with them when they are busy in an area of the house other than where we usually spend time. In these instances, I have often heard the special words that warm my heart, "Stay with me, Dandy." When they make this request, I put off anything else I want to do so I can remain with them. I remember an incident similar to these when our daughter, Mary, was their age. At the time, we lived in a neighborhood, and one of the neighbors had a large, rambunctious golden retriever named

Rusty that would frighten Mary. One day, we were walking along the street, and Rusty came toward us. Of course, Mary was worried that Rusty would bother her, and said as much. I remember telling her, "Don't worry about Rusty; I'm with you."

All of these experiences illustrate how we should be dependent on the presence of our Heavenly Father. Throughout my life, I have wanted to make sure that as I moved along, the presence of God was with me. In one instance, I was at something of a crossroads in my life and had to make a difficult career decision to resign from my job. One morning as I prayed, I had an experience in which I saw myself walking with Jesus through a garden. As we walked along, the Lord said, "Let's go this way." Immediately, we were in a very dark place, and it was there I heard the Lord say, "As long as I am with you, does it matter where we are?" I did go through a dark time, but I never doubted that He was guiding me through it. In my experience, there have been other dark times, and it was the presence of the Lord Jesus Christ that got me through them all. The Apostle Paul had a similar experience when everyone deserted him as he recounted in Second Timothy 4:17, "But the Lord remained by my side and gave me strength…." Knowing that we are in the presence of God is strengthening. But the great danger is that we should ever leave His presence and not realize what has happened.

There is a disturbing passage in Judges 16:20, "He was unaware that the Lord had departed from him." This is the well-known story of Samson and Delilah. In this story, Samson, who was a real-life

110

superhero, fell in love with a woman named Delilah. Unfortunately, she did not love him quite as much because she was willing to betray him for money. Following her repeated attempts to learn the source of his great strength, Samson finally gave in when she used that most effective phrase, "How can you say you really love me when you won't share your secrets with me?" Wow! Who could resist! Worn down with this incessant line of questioning, Samson finally gave in and told her that his long hair was the source of his strength. The result of giving up this secret was that while he slept, she shaved his head and surrendered him to his enemies, the Philistines. Initially, Samson thought he would escape, but as the passage states, "He was unaware that the Lord had departed from him." The Philistines were then able to capture and blind him. Then they took him prisoner for the purpose of essentially tormenting him.

In Samson's case, I believe he made the mistake of taking for granted that God would always be there to strengthen him when he needed it. Unfortunately, he placed himself in a dilemma of his own making. There may be times when God wants us to jump into the lion's den and then there are the times when it is wise to stay clear. As Jesus replied to Satan, in Matthew 4:7, "You will not deliberately do things in an attempt to move the Lord to action." In other words, don't go jumping off tall buildings and expect divine intervention. Another instructive instance is found in the story of King Hezekiah's miraculous recovery from a sickness.

In this story, found in Second Kings 20 and Second Chronicles 32, the prophet Isaiah told King Hezekiah that he would die as a result of sickness. However, when the king sincerely prayed, God told him, through Isaiah, that he would be given an additional fifteen years to live. As a sign that he would live, God caused the sun to move back in the sky. Following his recovery, the text in Second Chronicles 32:31 says that "God left Hezekiah for a while to see what was in his heart." The test came when envoys from Babylon came to visit Hezekiah and to investigate the sign that had occurred. Instead of praising God and focusing on all that God had done in his miraculous healing and the sun actually moving backward, Hezekiah showed them all his treasures. From this story, we can see a second way in which our God might leave us alone for a while.

These examples should make it clear that there are certain times in which we should know that God is not going with us. In the instance of Samson, he was cavorting with the enemy. Judges 16 begins by saying that Samson went to Gaza, a Philistine city, to see a prostitute. Then it says he loved a woman named Delilah in the valley of Sorek, which was also in Philistine territory. The lesson from Samson is that if we are willfully engaging in activities that are displeasing to God, there will come a point at which He will not be with us. Proverbs 28:9 says that "Whenever someone refuses to pay heed to the law, that person's prayer will be an affront to the Lord." In Samson's case, his association with the Philistines was prohibited by the law God gave to the Israelites.

In Hezekiah's life, at a time when he should have been dancing before the Lord with all his might, like King David, he was essentially boasting of his great wealth. We all enjoy talking about the things that we are most excited about. Hezekiah knew from the prophet Isaiah that he had been granted another fifteen years of life. On top of that, God performed a remarkable sign to confirm his healing. Still, these are not the only things God did for Hezekiah. One other remarkable event is recorded in Second Chronicles 32:9-23, when Sennacherib, King of Assyria, threatened Jerusalem. After Hezekiah and Isaiah prayed, the angel of the Lord struck down the Assyrian Army. Certainly, this was another opportunity to say, look what the Lord has done! But when the envoys from Babylon came to investigate why the sun went backward, Hezekiah showed them everything he had. It's like someone coming to you and wanting to learn about Jesus, and all you can talk about is your new car! By leaving Hezekiah alone, God saw what was really most important to him.

The scriptures are clear that God wants to be number one in each of our lives. There is no substitute. When we have the attitude of the Psalmist in 16:5, "The Lord is my entire inheritance and my supplier who takes care of everything," then we will be on our way to prizing the greatest, and only lasting treasure-our God. Psalm 91 is most comforting as it describes God's perfect protection of those who "dwell in God's shelter." When we keep God in our thoughts through meditating on scripture, praying, singing a song of worship in our minds, or just

113

thinking about Him, we are dwelling in His presence and can be thus assured that He is with us.

In the same way, as it is important that Debi and I be with JJ and Ella to provide assurance, our greatest desire should be that we are always in the presence of God Almighty. The only thing that will come between our God and us begins in our hearts and minds. Isaiah 26:3 puts it this way, "You, Lord, will give perfect peace to those of unwavering resolve, because their confidence is in You." As we resolve to trust in God and follow Him, like JJ and Ella, we are saying, "Stay with me, Father."

What About Him?

"When Peter looked at John, he asked Jesus, "Well, Lord, what about him?" Jesus then replied, "Even if I want him to live until My second coming, that is none of your business. Your business is to follow Me."" John 21:21-22

Children are quick to catch on to many things, but one thing they will never fail to notice is when another child gets something he or she does not have, to include extra attention from an adult. Even with their different interests, JJ and Ella frequently feel the other is receiving something extra. Sometimes they argue over a toy, a particular seat or

115

who gets to sit closest to Granny. This is human nature at its most predictable. I don't think any child wants to see another youngster receive more than he or she has, and as often happens when we adults see a friend or colleague promoted in some way we tend to think, "why him or her and not me?" Jesus dealt with this in the parable of the workers in Matthew 20:1-16. In this parable, Jesus describes a landowner who went out to find workers for his vineyard. The owner went out early in the morning and hired some workers. Then, throughout the day, the landowner continued hiring more workers to include some who worked for only one hour. At the end of the day, the employer paid everyone the same to include those who were hired last. As you might expect, those who worked all day grumbled about the inequity of the work to wages ratio, but the landowner reminded them that they received what they had agreed to. At its heart, this parable is about jealousy and the notion of fairness.

In our modern society, fairness is thought to be something of a cornerstone for civilized people. When most people think of fairness, they would describe it as everyone being treated the same without partiality. However, from a Biblical perspective, though He loves all of us equally, our Heavenly Father deals with everyone differently. The Apostle Paul considered this in First Corinthians 12-14 as he pointed out that God has given each of us different gifts. While the gifts, or talents, God has given us differ in prestige, they individually work together for the benefit of all. Moreover, as was the case between Peter and John, in John chapter 21, God has a different plan for each of us. The prophets of the exile provide a good illustration of this.

Daniel, Ezekiel, and Jeremiah were contemporaries at the time of the Babylonian siege of Jerusalem and subsequent exile, yet they each had very different experiences. Daniel was one of the early exiles to be taken to Babylon, and along with his friends Shadrach, Meshach, and Abednego, lived a somewhat privileged life in the palace, serving the King of Babylon. Ezekiel was also taken to Babylon but lived what we might think of as, at best, a middle-class existence among the other exiles. Jeremiah, however, was left in Jerusalem as a persecuted prophet. Each of these prophets endured hardship in different ways. God rescued Shadrach, Meshach, and Abednego from the fiery furnace; the Lord's angel protected Daniel in the lion's den. Ezekiel, on the other hand, was tasked with delivering God's word of judgment to the exiles, and the Lord allowed his wife to die for the purpose of making a point. While the prophets in exile were dealing with their different trials, Jeremiah was imprisoned, in the worst conditions, inside Jerusalem while it was under siege. Though he faithfully carried out the Lord's commands, no one listened to him, and after everyone else was carted off to Babylon, a band of renegades forced him to go with them to Egypt. Clearly, Jeremiah got the short end of the straw. So how is that fair? To our thinking, it is not fair at all.

If prominent Biblical characters were not, by our standards, treated fairly, I suspect there is something else at play here. The Key has to do with Jesus' reply to Peter in John 21:22. In this instance,

Jesus had just told Peter that someday he too would be crucified. This is not the kind of forecast any of us wants to hear. Since the Lord had said nothing about John's future, it seems natural for Peter to point to John and ask, "Well, what about him?" The essence of the Lord's answer was "Don't worry about My plans for him, just follow Me." When we begin to concern ourselves with our Father's plans for others, it is proof positive that we are not keeping our eyes on Him.

The first of the Ten Commandments in Exodus 20:2-3 is, "I am the Lord your God, and I alone delivered you from slavery in Egypt. You will not share your affections with any other god." Undoubtedly, our Heavenly Father wants to be number one in our lives. While the text indicates we are not to share our affections with other gods, I believe these can be anything that distracts us from what is really important. Such things can be money, possessions, relationships, and actually anything you can imagine. As the Lord spoke in Matthew 6:2, "your heart will be wherever your treasure is." So, according to this, whatever occupies my heart and is in my thoughts, that is my treasure. Are my thoughts on God and His kingdom or on something much less lasting? In this regard, the most tragic thing that we can do to ourselves is to let jealousy, envy, bitterness, and the like consume our thoughts. Those who give in to these temptations endanger their relationship with God and make this present life harder at the same time.

The Lord deals with each of us differently. Moreover, He does not explain to us the reasoning behind His every decision. His expectation is that we will "follow Him." The Old Testament character Job is the prime example. Following his sufferings and complaints, God Almighty answered him out of a whirlwind. Even though God spoke to him audibly, the Lord never told Job the reason for his suffering. I believe the lesson here is that God wants us to trust Him and know that He is concerned for us.

When JJ and Ella have their disagreements, Debi and I have found that it helps to redirect their attention toward us. When we can keep them occupied with what we are doing, or better, to have one of them help us do something, the rivalry disappears. This is the challenge for all of us. If we can keep our eyes on our Lord and refuse to be distracted by people, possessions, and events, we will be on our way to a deeper, more trusting relationship. In Revelation 2:17, Jesus tells the Church in Pergamum, "To whoever overcomes I will share My hidden food, and I will give that person a white stone with a new name written on it that no one knows except the person who receives it." While every person in the world may have a personal relationship with the Lord, our relationship with Him is meant to be ours and ours alone. Think about it; we each have our own unique relationship with God! This relationship is so unique, I once opined to a friend that it could be that when we see our Lord face to face, He could look different to each of us. Regardless of what the Lord looks like when we see Him, the best thing of all is that in this relationship, there is no lack and no fear of want. All we have to do is "follow Him."

119

Forgetting the Past

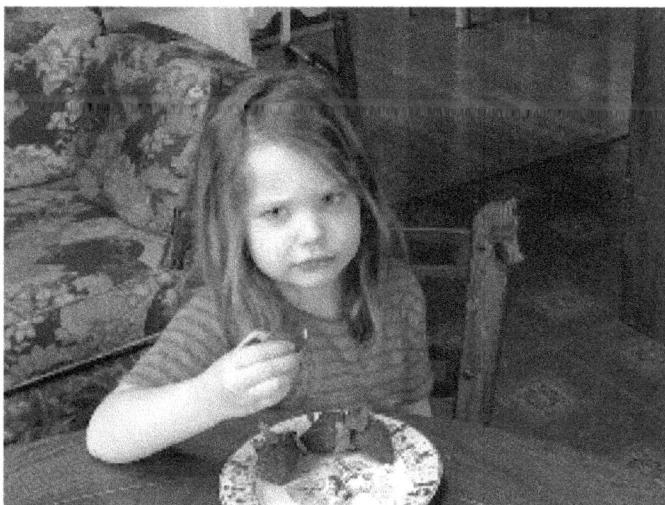

"Yes, O Lord, You will throw all our shortcomings into the very bottom of the sea." Micah 7:19

"East and west can never meet, and this is how far our God has removed our sins from us." Psalm 103:12

"I intentionally forget past achievements and press forward toward what is ahead." Philippians 3:13

There have been times when JJ and Ella have been, well, grouchy and said things that some people might find hurtful. There are rare times when Ella said something like, "I don't want to see you anymore," or "I don't like you anymore." Young children say these kinds of things, and thank God they quickly forget what they have said. Except for writing this chapter, I don't keep track of these things either. Because JJ and Ella are my grandchildren, I understand how it is, and these occasions do not come to mind. When I think of the children, I recall the best of times, of hugs, laughter, toys, and exploring something new. I understand that youngsters are liable to say just about anything. This is especially true when they are worn out from an eventful day. In these cases, the best parents and grandparents can do is "avoid upsetting the apple cart," as they say. It is interesting that following a nap or a good night's sleep, the children don't seem to have any remembrance of things they may have said or done, and neither do I. There are two tremendous lessons for us in this; our Heavenly Father forgets these things, and so should we.

The scriptures tell us that our Father has removed our sins from us as far as the east is from the west - an infinite distance that will never meet. The Bible also describes God's removal of our sins as having thrown them into the bottom of the sea, which is sometimes described as the sea of forgetfulness. We know from the scriptures that when our Heavenly Father sees us, He sees the righteousness of Jesus Christ. In this relationship, our sins are forgiven and washed away as if they never happened. To think that our Father sees us as perfect sons and daughters is more than an encouraging thought. However, the hard lesson for many of us is how forgetful we are regarding our shortcomings.

If our Heavenly Father completely forgets our faults and we are continually reminding Him, do you think His reaction might be something like, "What are you talking about?" For each of us to grow into the image of our Lord Jesus Christ, I believe it is reasonable to begin regarding ourselves as He considers us, perfect in every way. I've heard many testimonies about how our Lord rescued people from their sins. Sometimes, though, it seems as if Christians compete to have the greatest testimony. The person who was saved from the most impressive sin draws the biggest crowd. Then there have been times when Christians confess that they are saved, but they continue to carry the burden of their past. This is something that should not be, as the scriptures indicate that our past is something to be forgotten. It does not matter if you broke every commandment, built the world's largest company, or had the greatest ministry; except as milestones of God's faithfulness, don't keep looking in the rearview mirror!

Whether you are living in sorrow over the past or boasting about what you achieved, the only important consideration is becoming more like Jesus. Isaiah 43:18-19 has been a very important scripture to me throughout my adult life. Here, our Father speaks through the prophet, saying, "Don't keep thinking about things that have happened, and do not meditate on the past. Look, I am going to do something new, it's coming now; won't you take notice of it? I will go as far as to make a highway on impassable ground and a river in the driest desert." Our God and Father specializes in doing what we consider impossible! What is more impossible than a changed past? If we are to be transformed into His image, we have to forget our failures. With JJ and

Ella, every day is new. When they come to be with Debi and me, they are not bragging about what they have done (except, of course, for good grades), nor are they apologizing. They come expecting a loving embrace from us. The same relationship with God is available to everyone who trusts in Jesus. Yet as long as we agonize over the former problems, we will suffer unnecessarily and open the door to the possibility that we will return to that sin.

If we are meditating on, constantly remembering, past wrongs, where will the good thoughts come from? In this regard, Proverbs 23:7 states, "A person is made up of his or her thoughts." Based on this passage, I get the impression that if we continue to remember our sins, we will never escape them. Proverbs 26:11 describes the person who continues to repeat the same sin as a dog that keeps coming back to its own vomit. I do not want this description to fit me! The best way to escape transgressions that continue to entangle us is to consider ourselves dead.

In regard to considering ourselves dead, the Apostle Paul exclaimed in Galatians 2:20, "I am crucified with the Lord Jesus Christ; I am no longer alive rather Christ is living in me and this present life in the flesh I'm living by unwavering belief in God's Son who loved me so much that He gave up His life for me." I think we are called to be so forgetful that we lose sight of our own being. To do this we have to, as Paul said in Second Corinthians 10:5, "take absolute control over every thought in obedience to the Lord Jesus Christ."

The best way to take absolute control of every thought is to continuously meditate on scripture and pray. Paul wrote in Philippians 4:8, "At last, my family, I want you to always think on things that are true, honorable, right, pure, lovely, reputable, excellent, and praiseworthy." It comes down to more than thinking happy thoughts; we are to think God's thoughts, and He thinks we are pretty special. At first, this does take some effort, but it will soon become our very nature, and this is what it is all about: being transformed by the renewing of our minds! (Romans 12:2)

Like JJ and Ella, it is their nature to know that Debi and I love them and accept them at all times. Our acceptance of them is what they focus on, and God's acceptance of us should be our foremost thought.

Watching Father God Work

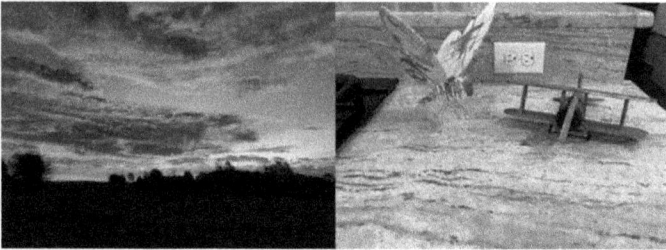

"The sky above is shouting about the awesomeness of God and is showing off His incredible work."
Psalm 19:1

As a grandfather, it has not been unusual to have my grandchildren sit in my lap, sometimes more than one at the same time. As they have grown a little older, this is less frequent. Still, not long ago, we were watching something on TV when my six-year-old grandson, JJ, walked over and sat in my lap. Usually, when one of the children sits with me, we are watching a favorite show on television. As I was praying one morning, I wondered, when we are sitting in our Heavenly Father's lap, what do we watch? The thought that came to my mind was that we watch God do what He does, which is make things new.

Over the years, I've come to realize that our Father is in the business of surprise. Very frequently, He lets us think we have got things figured out, and He does something else. Our Father always does something unexpected; He likes to surprise us. In Lamentations 3:22-23, the prophet Jeremiah wrote,

"My Lord's tender affections will never end because his intimate concern for me will never fail. They begin anew every single day! How awesome is Your faithfulness!" Jeremiah is referred to as the suffering prophet, yet in the midst of devastation and depression, he recognized that with God, every day is new and fresh. A chance to start over, if you will. In this regard, the Psalmist wrote in Psalm 19:1, "The sky above is shouting about the awesomeness of God and is showing off His incredible work." This Psalm goes on to describe how creation is itself a testament to God who made it.

Father God is also continuously active in His creation. In the book of Job, God confronted the suffering questioner and asked him, "When did you ever tell the new day to begin, and made daybreak to know when to come…?" (Job 38:12) Not only does He command the days and seasons, as the creator, He holds all things together. Hebrews 1:3 takes up this idea of God's intimate involvement in creation when it says, "From Jesus, God's glory is on full and magnificent display, and Jesus is the exact demonstration of God's nature and holds everything together by His powerful word."

The scriptures are full of references to our God's wondrous works. In this day and age, most people have seen the time-lapse photography or videos of everything from flowers blooming to butterflies breaking free from their cocoons. I suspect we will watch with amazement as Father does the most incredible things. As I was praying one morning I imagined a crystal flower blooming, which I don't think is at all farfetched and probably quite common where we are going. When Paul spoke of the Lord's coming in Second Thessalonians 1:10, he described our reaction to his appearing as "everyone who has believed will marvel at His glory." Essentially we will be struck with awe and wonder that we will never get used to because, as Jeremiah said, it will always be new.

I never get tired of making things for my grandchildren, and they sometimes make odd requests. After watching a documentary on the Red Baron, JJ asked me to make a Red Baron airplane for him. My granddaughter, Ella, was quick to add, I want a butterfly! Okay, the airplane I'm comfortable with, but a butterfly? As I worked on the biplane, which JJ painted red, I kept thinking about how I would make the butterfly. I finally figured out how to make a semblance of a butterfly for Ella. Like JJ's Red Baron plane, Ella painted her butterfly. I was surprised when my daughter, Mary their mother was impressed and posted pictures on social media saying, "Is there anything my dad can't make?? I mean, WOW!! What a talented Dandy my kiddos have!! JJ asked for a air plane, and Ella asked for a butterfly. My heart is full!" If Mary and the children can get excited about a couple of roughed-out toys, how much more full will our hearts be as we constantly watch Father God do the most wonderful things for us?

I'm pleased that Mary has grown to appreciate the things Father does. Not long ago, as the sun was setting, the sky was especially colorful. Again, Mary posted the picture on social media saying, "God was showing off a little I think. So beautiful!" I admit that my handmade toys are no match for Father's handiwork. As we consider these things and the awe-inspiring power of God that is on display each and every day, why do we ever worry? Jesus said it best when He noted that God feeds the birds of the air without them working at all, He clothes the flowers of the field more splendidly than royalty, so don't you think He will take care of you?

Perhaps the scriptures that celebrate God's visible creation are making the point that if we will take the time to watch what He is doing, we will grow more and more confident of His provision and protection. The problem is that often we get so used to our surroundings and we lose sight of the actual miracles that take place every day. Yet the more we appreciate the visible aspects of His creation, the more aware we will become of aspects that are not quite as visible. Whenever I hear a bird chirping, I hear it as Father God telling me He loves me. I respond to the sound of the birds, "I love You too." There are just so many things that He wants to show us, but we have to slow down and essentially, sit in His lap for a while to see these things. Once we become consumed with what He is doing, we probably won't have time to worry about anything else.

Nimrod the Mighty Hunter

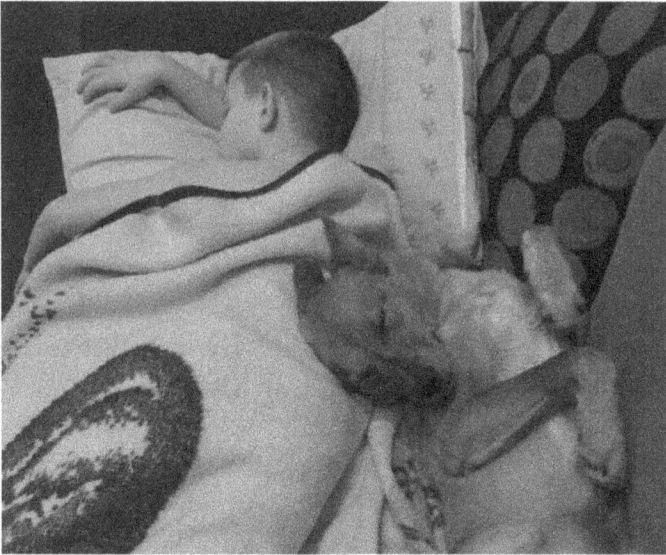

"There is no other god like you, O Lord, and there are certainly no deeds or creations like yours."
Psalm 86:8

"You are not to have any other gods before Me."
Exodus 20:3

Coming to our house after school became something of a tradition when JJ and Ella started attending classes. The weekday afternoons usually went the same way. Mary would leave to pick up the children at about 2:00, then around 2:30 the phone would ring, and a small voice would ask, "Can I come to your house?" Debi or I would almost always respond, "Of course you can." Then when JJ and Ella arrived they expected popcorn, a drink and want to either play a game, or watch a favorite movie. This became such a routine that on those occasions when they did not call, I was disappointed. Then along came Nimrod, the mighty hunter.

It was one weekend that Debi and I stopped by to see Mary, Jerry, and the children, and we were introduced to their new puppy. Mary wanted to give the puppy a Biblical name they all could agree on, so I recommended the name Boaz, as found in the book of Ruth, because my parents had a Boaz many years before. No one was very keen on the name Boaz. They were looking for a more powerful name, if you will. I figured Nebuchadnezzar was out of the question, so I suggested Nimrod the mighty hunter. This name stuck, though they just call him Nimrod. Following Nimrod's arrival, I soon noticed a change in JJ's behavior. He was not quite as interested in spending time with old Dandy.

I was surprised the first time Ella came alone to visit after school. As Ella opened the car door and stepped out, I asked JJ if he wanted to stay, and he replied, "I want to go see Nimrod." I was floored! Replaced by a puppy! Can you imagine? What young boy would rather play with his dog rather than his grandfather? As time went on JJ would still come around more but he still liked being with Nimrod. The thing I learned from this is that we do this very same thing to our Heavenly Father. I have learned over the years that He really does want to spend time with us and He wants us to desire to be in His presence.

Scripturally, God is looking for people who are looking for Him and want to be in His presence. Psalm 63 gives a pretty good example of what our Father is looking for as the Psalmist says, "I will intently look for You." The fact that in the Old Testament Israel was described as God's wife and in the New Testament the Church is designated as the "bride of Christ" should be a good indication of what He wants from us. He wants our constant attention.

Jesus set the example for us in the Gospels as he would go up a mountain or to a remote place to pray even after teaching all day (Mark 6:46). Jesus also slipped in another aspect of loving God when He quoted the greatest commandment in Matthew 22:37, "You are to love your God and Master with your entire heart, with the totality your soul and with every thought in your mind." The aspect that Jesus added was that of loving God with our entire mind, as Deuteronomy 6:5 says, "You are to love your God and Master with your entire heart and with the totality of your soul and with every ounce of strength you have." Jesus added our mind's activity into loving our Father. The Apostle Paul emphasized this to the churches when he encouraged them to "pray continuously," (First Thessalonians 5:17), and to "sing with thankfulness in their hearts to God." (Colossians 3:16). In Philippians 4:6-7, Paul told his readers, "Don't worry about anything, rather pray about everything, ask, and give thanks to God. When you do this, God's peace of mind will take over in your hearts and minds." The great thing about spending time in Father's presence is that no matter what is going on in our lives, we can have peace and be free from worry.

In spite of the assurances we have in the scriptures, we still tend to wander away from our great God who loves us so much. Think about the times you have purchased something special, and you've been obsessed with it. How many times have we gone to a movie or listened to music and praised the production to others, recommending they see or hear it as well? The list is endless, and it also includes work and family. Have you ever been too busy to pray? I confess that I have been guilty of this. However, this is not to say that we cannot enjoy these other things in our lives. Paul made it clear in First Timothy 4:4 that we are to enjoy God's provision with thanksgiving. This means if you get a new car or something you are excited about, you can still include God by giving thanks. Even in instances in which we are overwhelmed by work, there is always time to pray and ask for God's guidance.

Like Nimrod taking JJ's attention from me, there are so many things that divert our attention from the One who loves us most. I have to admit there are times when JJ wants to include me in his time with Nimrod. Having a very energetic puppy jump on me is not my idea of the most fun, but it is an effort on JJ's part to include me. Fortunately, our Heavenly Father is not burdened with such things the way we are. In our relationship with Him, He wants to be a part of our excitement. He wants us to enjoy the good things He has given us with thankfulness. He wants us to constantly come to Him with our problems and concerns. Essentially, He wants to be included in every aspect of our lives. So, what was the last thing you talked to God about?

When Life Gets Out of Control

"Don't be afraid, because I'm with you; don't nervously glance from side to side because I am your God. I will give you the strength you need, and I will certainly help you. Do not doubt that I will hold you up with my own righteous right hand." Isaiah 41:10

It was a cool and pleasant fall afternoon, and I decided to do a little fall cleaning in the garage. In order to get to some things, I had to move the mower and a few other items. Anyone who knows JJ understands that he was born to drive. So, it should be no surprise that he quickly sat on the mower and asked if he could start it. Yes, I knew this was leading to the next question. "Go ahead," I told him. When he turned the key, it was clear it wasn't getting enough gas, so I increased the throttle and choked it for him. Sure enough, it quickly started, and he wanted to drive it around, so I thought "what the heck," and let him go. However, I forgot that it was still throttled up! There I was, the thoughtful grandfather, watching my six-year-old grandson eagerly push the control bars forward causing the front of mower to lift off the ground like a stallion about to race. From that point he darted across the yard in every direction. "Yikes!" While Mary was laughing herself silly and working feverishly to video her old dad having a nervous breakdown, I was yelling, "Stop, stop, stop!" as JJ raced back and forth with the biggest grin you could imagine. After a few harrowing moments, JJ did steer the mower back to us so I could slow it down, but not before I nearly had a heart attack. I can now laugh at this but it is an example of how sometimes life can get out of control.

We all like to say that we are in charge of our lives or that we make our own luck, but the fact of the matter is there are few things that we actually have control over. For most of my adult life, I exercised and maintained a sensible diet to stay in good physical shape. I thought I would be young forever. However, that did not preclude inevitable injuries from time to time and the fact that in spite of all that effort, today I look like a typical sixty-five-year-old. There are so many other things over which we have little to no influence, such as severe weather, the state of the economy, wars, criminal activity, and just plain old wear and tear to the equipment we use. We live in a world where "moth and rust spoils and where thieves come in and steal." (Matthew 6:19).

Depending on a persons' situation it is enough to make one fearful. However, for those who have a relationship with God through our Lord Jesus Christ, we are told not to be fearful.

There were several times that Jesus told the disciples to "fear not." The story that comes immediately to mind is Luke 8:22-25. In this instance, Jesus and the disciples got into a boat to go to the other side of the lake. As they were making their way across the water and a storm came up, fierce enough that it was filling the boat with water and, understandably, frightened the disciples. This is as good an example of life out of control as I can think of. Think about it. You are in the middle of a large body of water the wind is about to blow the boat over, it is about to sink and even if you can swim, you can't do so in such a storm. What do you do?! Fortunately for the disciples, Jesus was with them but he was asleep. How can anyone sleep under such conditions? I can see it now, the disciples grab Jesus shouting, "We're going to die, we're going to die!" Jesus then stretches, maybe yawns and says, "Wind and waves, be calm!" Then He looks at the disciples and essentially says, "What's the big deal?"

Each one of us goes through the storms of life often thinking, "This is the big one!" and we ask, "Where is God?" Like the disciples in the boat, He is right there with us knowing that what seems major to us is no great matter to Him. The reason is that He knows you will not sink and He will not let the wind blow you over. The disciples were in no danger as long as Jesus was with them even if He was asleep. In our case, we have the promise that our God does not slumber or sleep as He watches over us, Psalm 121:3-4. Moreover, Jesus Himself said He is with us always to the end of the age, Matthew 28:20. So, in a sense, we are like the disciples as we go through these storms of life thinking that we are about to be swamped when our God is with us all the time.

I have learned from personal experience that even when it seems our boat has not come in but rather has sunk, our God can still make it happen. The greatest example of this is the story of Lazarus in John Chapter 11. In this story, Jesus learns that His friend Lazarus is sick but rather than immediately going to heal him, He waits a couple of days. By the time Jesus arrives, Lazarus has been dead for four days. So, everyone seems to know who Jesus is and they're wondering, "Why didn't Jesus heal His friend?" Well, they were about to get the answer when Jesus had them remove the stone and commanded Lazarus to come out! Notice what Jesus did? He let a situation become hopeless so He could work an incredible miracle. God never does anything that is easy!

In my life, the Lord has allowed me to go through some disappointments so that He could bring about something greater. Even in the times when I could not see a greater outcome, I can now look back and see the growth that the Lord brought about in my life. Don't you think that the disciples in the boat gained a little more faith after seeing Jesus calm the wind and the waves? The same can be true for each of us as we go through these storms. We just have to remember who is in control.

Written For Us

Ella, Miss Ella
Miss Honeysuckle Rose
Loves to dance
On her toes.

*"Father, You watched as I took form in the womb,
and You had already written of my entire life before
I was born."* Psalm 139:16

One of the things I love to do is write poems and jingles for my children and now grandchildren. I suppose this may seem like a strange hobby to some, but for me it comes as naturally as water flowing down a mountain stream. It's just what I do. Some of the ditties I write are quite catchy, at least to me. For example, there was "CJ the blue jay," "Big Mike" and for Mary, "Princess Pea" after the story of the princess and the pea. For each nickname there was an accompanying rhyme. Sometimes the children were not impressed, but it gave me pleasure because I love them so much. With grandchildren I have continued with this tradition. As I was sitting in church one Sunday, it occurred to me that our

138

Heavenly Father loves to do the same for each of us. Incredible as it may seem, He is so intimate with each of us that He has already written a book about us! Psalm 139 says so. I realize that for some people this gets into the idea of predestination and there is nothing we can do about it, but I prefer to think of it as, "Wow! What have You written for me today?!"

We all think about the things that are most important to us. However, I believe that when we go from thinking about someone to writing or composing it brings the relationship to an entirely different level. When I was a young captain in the Air Force I had to travel from Japan to the United States for a two-month school. Debi and the children of course remained in Japan. This was before emails and cheap phone calls, so I wrote home every day. Because, of the nature of what we now refer to as snail mail, Debi was receiving my letters even after I got back home. The important thing for me at this time was that I wanted Debi and the children to know I was always thinking of them. During this period there were many things going through my mind such as good pizza, ice cream and school related activities, but I did not write about any of these things except in my letters home and certainly not in an affectionate way. I believe that our Heavenly Father writes about us in an affectionate way and that He sees only the best in us. Psalm 56:8 is a good passage to support this belief; "You, Father have considered my comings and goings; You put my tears in Your bottle, and You wrote them in your book." This tells me that He is keeping track of the things we forget. After I completed From the Mouths of Babes, I was very pleased when Mary told me she was reading it. The thing that touched me most was when she said she did not remember some of the things I had written about her. These remembrances brought tears to her eyes to think that I kept up with such things. Hey, this is how our Heavenly Father thinks about us!

Not only does our Father keep up with the tears we cry, according to Matthew 10:30 and Luke 12:7 the hairs of our heads are numbered. In my case, being bald makes this easy to keep up with. Yet the real lesson is that our Father thinks of us constantly at a level of detail that is incomprehensible. I come from an agricultural family that raises livestock, so I can appreciate Proverbs 27:23 which admonishes those with livestock to pay attention to the condition of their flocks and herds. The authors of Proverbs would give the same advice to home builders; "pay attention to the quality of the materials you are using" for example. However, whether raising livestock, building homes or any other endeavor, none of us would go into the detail Father God does regarding our lives.

I believe the ultimate written expression of the Father's love for us is The Song of Solomon. I do confess that of all the books in the Bible this is my least favorite, but I need to look at it from another perspective. Many people think of this short book as an allegory about Christ's love for the Church and after some reflection I agree. Our Father is writing about each of us in affectionate ways, looking forward to the moment we are joined together with Him in glory.

At the same time that our Father wants us to be with Him and desires to write good things about us, we have a choice to make. This is where I think we get away from the predestination problem. Either we can write our own book, or we can let our Father write it. If we choose to go at it on our own the story we will produce will be filled with everything we have done. Think about this for a minute. Do you want Father God to open the books and see everything you have done? Not me! On the other hand He offers to write our book for us. When we trust in Jesus Christ as our Savior and Lord, we are accepting His righteousness in place of our own. So, when Father God writes our story, He is writing about Jesus! There is a good example in the Old Testament that illustrates the difference between who writes the story.

Take a look at Second Samuel chapter 11, which recounts the story of David committing adultery with Bathsheba and his subsequent murder of Uriah, Bathsheba's husband. It is spelled out in all the shocking details for the world to see. Now compare this narrative to First Chronicles 20, which details the same period in David's life. There is no mention of the affair at all-like it never happened! This is the difference between us writing our own story and letting Father God write it for us. When we turn our lives over to the Lord Jesus, He completely rewrites our story so that we look like Him.

In addition to replacing our faults with Jesus' blamelessness, Father God has a detailed plan for our lives that we can live out as long as we are surrendered to His will. This doesn't necessarily mean we will be rich and famous, but it does mean we will be living the life He wants us to have. So, I say again, what has Father God written for me today?!

Not Now

"Guide me to walk according to Your truths and let me learn them, because You are my God and salvation and I excitedly wait for You all day long." Psalm 25:5

"There is a designated stage for everything. And there is an appropriate moment for everything that takes place in this world." Ecclesiastes 3:1

"And Jesus said to His mother, "Why do you want to involve Me? It is not yet My time."" John 2:4

"Now when time had reached its peak, God sent His Son into the world through natural childbirth and under the Mosaic Law." Galatians 4:4

Being retired as we are, Debi and I have a daily routine. Debi doesn't mind being pulled away from her normal schedule, but I am, well, a little obsessive-compulsive in the way I do things. With this said, you can imagine that with JJ and Ella nearby, we are frequently interrupted. It was a bright, early August morning when Ella excitedly came running into the kitchen to tell us that she had learned to ride her bike without training wheels. "That's wonderful," Debi and I both exclaimed. "Come watch me ride," was her follow-on command. *Are you kidding?* I thought. *We haven't even eaten breakfast yet!* So my answer was, "We will come later on today, but we have some things to do first." As you might imagine, this did not sit well with an excited five-year-old. Ella left with her mom, Mary, but she was not what we refer to as a happy camper. I never want to disappoint my children in any way, so this bothered me, but I realized there was a deeper truth to this incident.

The pastor and a few of us meet for lunch weekly to share what the Lord is doing in our lives. This is generally a light-hearted opportunity to encourage and learn from each other. One of my frequent comments has been, "Our Father never does things the way we think He should." Please keep in mind that when I say this, it is not a complaint but a statement of fact spoken in such a way as to cause laughter. Still, if you think about it, this is a statement of fact. Our Heavenly Father doesn't do things the way we wish He would, and He doesn't work on our timetable.

When it comes to waiting, I think I have more experience than most. When I was on active duty in the Air Force, I had to wait longer than usual for my promotions. In the armed forces, when someone is promoted, it does not mean they get to pin on the new rank right away. No, each person selected for advancement is given a line number based on longevity. In other words, the person who has been in the longest gets to pin on the soonest. In my case, my commissioning date was at the end of November, so that meant I was at the back of the bus. I had to wait 19 long months to pin on major and 21 months to pin on lieutenant colonel. Believe me, there were times I forgot that I was ever selected for promotion! Advancement was not the only thing I had to wait for.

I have loved writing for many years and especially writing on Biblical subjects. I wrote several articles hoping to be published in Christian publications, with no results. I remember one day sitting at the dinner table saying, "I don't know why the Lord does not open a door for my writing." My son CJ, who was about ten at the time said, "Maybe God wants you to be in the Air Force." Talk about from the mouths of babes! CJ's comment got my attention and as you can see, I have never forgotten it.

Biblically, those who seek after God have had to wait for what they were called to, and in many cases, this has been a significant length of time. First, we have Abraham and Sarah, who had to wait until very old age before they were given their promised son, Isaac. Joseph, through no fault of his own, was enslaved and spent years in prison before becoming ruler of Egypt. Then there is Moses, who spent forty years herding sheep in the desert before God called him to deliver Israel from bondage in Egypt. David is another example, as he was anointed king, performed a significant feat in slaying the giant Goliath, and then spent a number of years as a fugitive running for his life. There are many other stories like these in the scriptures, but the point is that our Heavenly Father makes his children wait for what He has promised. While we cannot know with certainty all of Father God's reasons, we can look at the results of the waiting.

In the case of Abraham, he grew in faith as he waited for God to fulfill His promise. In Romans 4:19-21, Paul said of Abraham, "Even though he was nearly 100 years old and together with Sarah, who was way beyond childbearing, were feeble in their bodies, having one foot in the grave, he never doubted God's promise. Rather, he grew in his faith and glorified God because he was convinced that God was more than able to achieve what He had promised." Our Father knew beforehand that Abraham would not fall into doubt, but this exercise had the effect of demonstrating to Abraham that he had the faith, and more importantly, his example remains as a testament to us today. A great lesson for believers throughout history has been Joseph.

In Romans 8:28 Paul wrote, "Now we know that God causes every event to work together to result in a good ending for those who love Him and He calls into His service." When I read this passage, Joseph jumps out as the quintessential example. In his case, we might look at his experience with a sour expression, and indeed, he experienced hardship, but our Father placed him right where he needed to be for the promotion that was prepared beforehand for him. In the case of Moses, he also had to experience some hard knocks.

As recorded in Acts 7:25, Moses thought that the Israelites would recognize that he was there to be their deliverer. Instead, they saw him as just a murderer. The 40 years he spent with the sheep taught him humility. In fact, Numbers 12:3 states that Moses was the most humble man on the earth. As First Peter 5:6 says, "Be humble under the powerful hand of God so that He can raise you up at just the right time." When we realize just how powerless we are, as Moses learned, we have no choice but to humbly wait on Him. King David also learned this the hard way.

Imagine, knowing God had selected you for a high position and someone else is keeping you from it for an extended period of time. You might feel helpless and ask, "What gives?" I know I would. At a very young age David had achieved some very heady feats. He killed a lion and a bear while protecting his sheep, he slew a fearsome giant everyone else was afraid to face, and, among other things, he was an accomplished musician. You might say he was a rock star! All this might have a tendency to go to your head, and I can confidently say it would have been that way with me. Because David had to flee from King Saul for several years, he learned total dependence on God and humility. Moreover, it was during this period that he wrote many of the Psalms that are such a blessing to us today.

In every case, those who waited extended periods for the fulfillment of God's promise received something far greater than they could have imagined. In his own power, could Moses part the Red Sea or, much less, feed all the people of Israel? He, like Abraham, Joseph, and David, had to wait longer than he would have liked, but the results were spectacular. So, what are you waiting for?

The Small Things

"Our Father loves us so much, He gives to us even while we are sleeping." Psalm 127:2

Let me be clear! When it comes to any sport or any activity requiring a sense of rhythm, I have two left feet. That is not to say I don't enjoy some aspects of sports. When my sons, CJ and Michael, were growing up, I enjoyed throwing a football with them. In fact, it was CJ who showed me how to properly throw a football. I know some of you are snickering, but I have talents in other areas. That said, I had begun thinking that it would be fun to throw the football back and forth with JJ. I used to have a very nice football, but I was unable to find it, so the thought slipped my mind. It wasn't long, though, until one afternoon JJ came walking up the

149

driveway with a football under his arms. What a delight! We had great fun throwing the ball back and forth to each other, and for once in my sporting life, I was able to give him some pointers. As you know, I treasure these times, and as I thought on it, I realized this was the fulfillment of an unspoken desire.

As I look back over my life, it has been filled with the granting of desires I never even asked for. Following my stint in the Navy many years ago, I returned home for a brief time and prepared for college. Something I had thought would be a joy was to live again with my parents and siblings as we had before I left home. The following summer, I decided not to go to summer school, but work at the family business for the term, and my desire was granted. What a delight it was to live again with the entire family for that summer. Then, when I retired from the Air Force, I thought it would be nice to have a job involving travel around the world. Little did I realize that I would begin working for the State Department and spend two years traveling to a different country every week! Again, I never asked for this; my Heavenly Father gave it to me. There have been other realized dreams like this. Each time it was like my Heavenly Father saying, "Here is a little something extra for you."

In our lives, we so often focus on the big things and achieving the major dreams in our hearts that we completely miss the little blessings that amount to a joyful life. The Sixteenth Century French Monk, known as Fenelon, wrote a book entitled *The Existence of God*. In his treatise, Fenelon argues from what we know of creation that God does exist. When I read his book, I was surprised at the depth he goes into to make his argument. For example, he spends a considerable amount of time describing the intricacies of the eye and the gift of sight. He also describes the tongue and discusses smell, taste, and hearing. It has occurred to me that our Father could have created us without the sense of taste or smell. When I think of this and my favorite foods and scents, I have to say, "Thank you, Father, for the gifts of taste and smell." We could add to this the gift of seeing in color. As I write, it is the fall season, my favorite, and the colorful foliage is at its peak. I love seeing the yellows, oranges, reds and greens in all their various shades. Like the universe itself, fall foliage is a heavenly work of art!

How many times do we go through our daily lives without giving thought to these small things that make our lives so enjoyable? In Matthew 5:45, Jesus said, "Our Heavenly Father makes the warming sun to shine on bad people as well as good, and He makes the good rain to come down on those who walk with upright integrity and those who do not." The Apostle Paul mentioned something similar in Acts 14:17, where he said, "Father God made Himself evident in that even when you refused to acknowledge Him, He was gracious to you and gave you rain that brought forth bountiful harvests that made you happy with good food to eat and cheerfulness." As I read passages like these, I'm inclined to consider that the real problem is that we take such things for granted and forget that these are things for which we should be giving thanks.

Psalm 100:4 encourages us to, "Come into Father's gates with thanksgiving and then into his royal courts with praise." This is the way we need to approach the God who loves us so much. When we take time to take stock of the little things we so often don't even think about and give thanks to our Father for them, it is a sure sign that we are drawing closer to Him. In my own prayer life, I've noticed that when I honestly count my blessings and give thanks for them, the follow-on response is one of praise to our Heavenly Father. Wow! Father, you gave me the taste to enjoy that meal I just finished, or thank you so very much for giving me the time to throw the football with JJ! A thankful heart will take us through Heavenly gates and bring us with praise into His courts.

While I try not to notice, I can't help but recognize when people fail to say thank you. Old fashioned as I am, I was raised to say please and thank you, and I can't help but notice these things. Yet those who touch me most are the ones who express gratitude. In such cases, I want to do more. Years ago, we were vacationing with Debi's parents at their lake house, and we went out and rented a jet ski. My brother-in-law brought a young man along who was about CJ's age, and we let him ride on the craft. I was overwhelmed by his expression of thanks for being able to join us. I believe this is the case with our Heavenly Father. The more we express our thankfulness to Him in even the smallest of things, the more He wants to reveal to us and give to us.

If you want to draw closer to Father God in a fresh and new way, begin giving thanks for the smallest of things. King David's recognition and thankfulness for all God has done resulted in the twenty-third Psalm! Who knows what Father God will do in your life as you focus on all His blessings for you.

When All Is Said and Done

JJ, Ella and Mary

"You, Lord will show me the way of true life, for in your presence is complete happiness, and in your right hand are everlasting pleasures." Psalm 16:11

"Where else can we go, Lord? Only you have words of everlasting life." John 6:68

Life in the modern world is something of a whirlwind for most of us. There is never enough time for everything that we consider to be important. As I have previously noted, in my retired state, I now have the opportunity to spend quality time with JJ and Ella. Since they have started going to school, I expect a call from them every afternoon asking if they can come to our house. Whenever they come, it makes for a fitting ending to the day, whether we throw a frisbee, play ball, or watch a movie. What we are doing is making memories that I hope will survive

154

with them long after Debi and I are gone. What amounts to making happy remembrances based on time with JJ and Ella is far more lasting in our relationship with our Heavenly Father. The times we spend with Him are moments of building our everlasting home.

When I was in graduate school, I wrote my master's thesis on Ecclesiastes and actually translated the book from the original Hebrew. There was one particular passage (7:2) that was especially puzzling to me: "It is preferable to spend time in a place of bereavement than to participate in a place of feasting, simply because this will come upon all of us and we need to take it to heart." Years ago, I remember seeing the bumper sticker that read, "He who dies with the most wins!" There is a great underlying truth to this statement, which is analogous to a joke I once heard: "How much did this rich person leave behind?" Answer: "All of it." These are not just witticisms; they are an acknowledgment that there is something much greater than anything we can achieve in our lives. To some people, this greater thing is a lasting legacy or death itself. To others of us, it is not a thing but who; God Almighty. Yet, another point here is that there are certain things that lose relevance to us throughout our lives.

Watching JJ and Ella grow up reinforces what Debi and I saw as we raised our children. There are toys and possessions they value now but will grow tired of in time. When JJ was just under a year old, while Mary and Jerry were still living with us, Debi bought a "Thomas the Train" riding toy. Debi always gets up before me, and I have wonderful memories of waking up to a child's tune that the train would play as JJ pushed it around. As much as JJ loved this toy, he outgrew it, along with his rocking horse and many other toddler toys. The same is true for us; we outgrow or lose interest in things as we grow older. For many years, I identified myself by the car I drove, a two-seat roadster. Now I am very happy driving a rather bland SUV that I can easily get in and out of. So what lasts?

For most readers, to ask what lasts is a rhetorical question, as I'm sure you will answer that our relationship with God is the only thing that lasts. Jesus said in Matthew 6:19-21, "Don't store up worldly treasures that are easily destroyed by insects and degradation, and are at risk to thievery, rather store your treasures in heaven where there are no problems with destructive insects or corrosion, and there are no thieves, because your heart is going to be wherever your treasure is." In the chapter "All This is Ours," I presented my belief that the riches of the universe are ours through our Lord Jesus Christ, and noted the possibility that Father God could actually give us our own galaxy. When I think of having something of this magnitude, my next thought is, "What now?" Solomon made an astute observation in Ecclesiastes 5:11, "When there is an abundance of good things, there will be more people to make use of them. So what is the big deal for those who purchase these things, except to enjoy looking at them?" As I have mentioned, my home study is filled with memorabilia from a life of world travels. However, I must admit, as I sit working at my desk, these things are far from my thoughts. So how much thought will I devote to my heavenly possessions? Maybe not as much as one would think!

Throughout this book, I have described the joys of being with JJ and Ella. Except for watching them enjoy their toys or seeing JJ ride his four-wheeler, the joy has been in the time together. Based on this, I conclude that the joy of heaven will be continuous time together. Jude 24 is a passage that has particular meaning to me: "Now to the One who is able to protect you from stumbling and to present you in the presence of His magnificence with unimaginable excitement." Many years ago, I had an experience that I could not explain except by this passage. For a brief moment, I was in a brilliant white room filled with people and felt a sense of purity and excitement that was indescribable. I've read of other people with similar experiences and have to conclude this is what it is all about: the joy of being together with others in His presence.

As we spend time in our Father's presence, we are practicing for what is to come. No achievement in this life can compare to the joy and excitement we have to look forward to. Based on what I've learned over the years, our closeness to Him then will be based on our closeness now. Essentially, time spent in God's presence is the equivalent of storing up our treasures in heaven. Moreover, as 1 John 2:28 says, "My young children practice being in His presence so if He should suddenly come, we can have confidence rather than shamefully pulling away from Him at His arrival." It all has to do with how well we know Him.

If we grow in our relationship with God our Father through the Lord Jesus Christ, we will have the same confidence as JJ and Ella when they come expectantly into Debi's and my house. We can confidently eat from His plate, claim His creation as ours, play in His presence, and love Him with our entire being. While Debi and I only have nine grandchildren who can come with this confidence, heaven's doors are open to every human being who will let Jesus clothe them with His righteousness. Perhaps the most appropriate way to sum it all up is found in Revelation 22:17, "Both the Holy Spirit and the bride are calling, "Come." And whoever hears this, say "Come." And if anyone is thirsty come; for whoever wishes can drink the water of life free of charge." Come.

When There Is No One at the Door

"When the father saw his lost son in the distance, coming toward him, he couldn't help himself; he was so overwhelmed with loving joy, he raced to meet the young man and embraced him." Luke 15:20

As I write, it has been nine years since I began writing these vignettes about my grandchildren. Having raised three children through adolescence and into adulthood, I knew the day would come when our grandchildren were no longer interested in Debi and me. Little ones who were always talking suddenly became silent and more often than not gave one-word answers to questions. This is just the way it seems to be with most children when they reach their teen years.

In Jesus' story of the prodigal son, once the son came to his senses and returned home, the father was the one who saw him from a distance and ran to embrace him. (Luke 15:11-32). While there are fewer calls to come visit us and they no longer want to spend the night, like the father in the Lord's story, we are still alert to their call. Not long ago, our oldest granddaughter, Tristan, was working in an area not far from here and stopped by to spend the night with us a couple of times on her return trip home. You have to be a grandparent to understand this, but it was like Christmas came early to be with her. Each time we would go out to breakfast with her, and we would listen to her describe all the things going on in her life. What simple, yet wonderful memories!

So, if we enjoyed hearing about what is going on in our granddaughter's life, how interested in our lives is God? According to Matthew 10:29-31, God the Father is watchful of the birds of the sky and knows the number of hairs on our head. This tells me that He is concerned about the smallest details of our lives. There is nothing too insignificant to bring to Him. Moreover, Paul wrote that we should pray about all things. (Philippians 4:5-6).

The scriptures have much to say about prayer. The Lord said we should always pray and not become weary of seeking the Father. There are, however, a few things to avoid. When it comes to prayer, the Lord, Jesus, warned us to avoid formal and lengthy prayers spoken to impress listeners. (Matthew 6:5). He also warned us not be haughty in our prayers like the Pharisee, who prayed about how good he was. (Luke 18:9-12). The Epistle of James addresses the issue of praying for things to satisfy our own desires. (James 4:3). On the other side of the issue was the sinner in Luke 18:13 who very simply prayed, "Lord, deal kindly with me, a sinner."

When I speak with my children and grandchildren, there is no need for them to impress me. I'm already impressed. What I like to hear about is what is going on in their lives. Our grandson, Brandon, is in the Navy, and we love to hear about his adventures and how well he is doing in his career. JJ plays baseball and is a pitcher. It brings us great joy to hear about his pitching. (He strikes them out one after another!) Kensly is a beautician, and we enjoy knowing how much she enjoys her work. We are interested in everything they have to tell us. By the same token, our Father in heaven is interested in everything we have to tell Him. According to the scriptures, He already knows everything (Matthew 6:25-34), yet He wants us to talk to Him about it.

The importance of prayer comes back to having a relationship in which we are comfortable in the Lord's presence. Our pastor sometimes describes seeing congregants in the grocery store who have not attended church in a while. In these cases, he notes their tendency to turn away and act like they did not see him. Obviously, they do not feel comfortable in the pastor's presence. If we don't feel comfortable in the presence of a pastor, how can we ever be comfortable in the presence of Almighty God? A relationship is built on spending time together.

I have written about how comfortable JJ was eating off my plate as a toddler. He hasn't done this in many years now, but I would not mind if he did because he is my grandson and I love him. We are God's children, whom He created in His image. Moreover, when we believe in Jesus Christ as our Lord and Savior, He then fills us with His Holy Spirit. Thus, God the Father wants us to be comfortable and at home in His presence. This comfort comes in three ways: prayer, time spent reading the Bible, and fellowship with other believers in Jesus Christ. When we neglect these opportunities to draw near to God, we lose the opportunity to grow in our relationship with Him. If we neglect these things for a prolonged period, we will likely not be comfortable seeking to renew the relationship.

The wonderful thing is that, like the father in the story of the prodigal son, our Heavenly Father is waiting at the door watching for us to return and tell Him everything that is going on in our lives. Our grandchildren will always be welcome in our home, and as long as we are able, we will have a room prepared for them. The same is true with our Heavenly Father. Let's not keep Him waiting at the door.

About the Author

JJ and Dandy circa 2016

John C. (Chris) Orndorff is a retired Air Force Lieutenant Colonel and Special Agent with the Air Force Office of Special Investigations. His career includes four years in the Navy, 20 years in the Air Force, two years conducting antiterrorist activities for the US State Department, and 12 years teaching Air Force JROTC. Though his work centered around military activities, he studied to be a pastor and continues to have a passion for Biblical studies and education. He now volunteers his time to the Church and other conservative causes. While on active duty he was widely published in the military community and has written several books:

163

Prince Michael and the Dragon

Prince John's Quest

Princess Mary and the Prophet

Terrorists, Tornados and Tsunamis: How to Prepare for Life's Danger Zones

How Have the Mighty Fallen

The Gilgamesh Epic

The Enduring Art of War: A Paraphrase and Commentary on Sun Tzu

From the Mouths of Babes: Growing Closer to God Through Children

Great Trees from Little Acorns Grow: A History of Grace Baptist Church, Springfield, Tennessee 1927-2022

Solomon's Quest for the Meaning of Life: A Study of Ecclesiastes

The Journey

If you have enjoyed this book please let Chris know at chrisorndorff007@gmail.com . He would love to hear from you.

www.ingramcontent.com/pod-product-compliance
Lightning Source LLC
LaVergne TN
LVHW041221080426
835508LV00011B/1026